PROTECTING CHILDREN

PROTECTING CHILDREN

CLEVELAND TO ORKNEY: MORE LESSONS TO LEARN?

Proceedings of a one day conference organised by

Children in Scotland and the
National Children's Bureau

Edited by Stewart Asquith

Children
IN SCOTLAND
CLANN AN ALBA
working for children and their families

EDINBURGH: HMSO

Children in Scotland
Princes House
5 Shandwick Place
Edinburgh
EH2 4RG

TEL: 031 - 228 8484
FAX: 031 - 228 8585

ISBN 0 11 494262 5

CONTENTS

ACKNOWLEDGEMENTS

Editing the proceedings of a conference is never an easy task involving as it does considerable coordination, patience and perseverance on all sides. The task however was made considerably easier through the efforts of a number of key people without whom this book would not have appeared. The staff at Children in Scotland are to be congratulated on organising the conference and in particular, Annie Gunner in ensuring that the contributors, within tolerable limits, kept to the various deadlines. Laura Lochhead and Debbie McNab at the Centre for the Study of the Child and Society at the University of Glasgow had the unenviable task of transcribing the taped proceedings. Laura in particular bore the bulk of the work and also worked through the various drafts and corrections with her usual good humour. The book would not have been produced without the involvement of those mentioned. Nevertheless, any editorial mistakes and oddities must remain my responsibility.

STEWART ASQUITH

Please note, at the time of the conference on which this book is based, Children in Scotland was known as Scottish Child and Family Alliance (SCAFA). References to the organisation in the text have therefore been altered appropriately.

FOREWORD

In November 1992, Children in Scotland and the National Children's Bureau jointly organised a conference to examine the implications of Lord Clyde's *Report of the Inquiry into the Removal of Children from Orkney in February 1991*, which had been published the previous month. This book is based on contributions and discussions held at that conference.

The conference had been organised to look at the implications of the Clyde Report in the light of earlier inquiries, notably the *Report of the Inquiry into Child Abuse in Cleveland in 1987*, headed by Lord Justice Butler-Sloss, and to ask whether all the lessons of such inquiries had been learned. It also took place at a time when developments in the field of child law in Scotland were gathering pace; the Orkney Report took its place among many other reports on child law and related areas actively being considered by the government in the preparation of children's legislation for Scotland.

The conference, which was chaired by Lord Morton of Shuna, Chair of Scottish Child and Family Alliance, and Barbara Kahan, Chair of the National Children's Bureau, was attended by members of all the professions involved in child protection work and the care of children – social work, education and health professionals, lawyers, Children's Panel members, police officers, reporters – as well as researchers, local authority elected members, voluntary agencies, and representatives of most of the key agencies and groups involved in the Orkney affair itself, including parents.

This book is an important record of that day. It provides the full texts of all the contributions from the platform, the edited transcripts of the discussion that followed each speaker, and an immensely useful introduction by Professor Stewart Asquith, himself a contributor, setting the proceedings in context.

As child protection goes through changes recommended after Cleveland and Orkney; as the impact of the Children Act 1989 in England and Wales is assessed; and as Scotland moves nearer to comprehensive legislation on child care, this book is a valuable record of the thinking behind the legislation and the concerns of the key agencies who will, as Lord Justice Butler-Sloss puts it, be 'at the coalface' of child protection work.

LORD MORTON OF SHUNA,
Chair of Scottish Child and Family Alliance

PETER C. MILLAR OBE WS
Convener of Children in Scotland

CONTRIBUTORS

The Rt. Hon. **Lord Clyde QC,** Chairman of the Orkney Inquiry was called to the Scottish Bar in 1959, became a QC in 1971 and was Advocate Depute from 1973–4. He was a judge of the Courts of Appeal of Jersey and Guernsey from 1979–85, and since 1985 has been Senator of the College of Justice. He has also been Chairman of the Medical Appeals Tribunal 1974–85; Chairman of the Committee of Investigation for Scotland on Agricultural Marketing, 1984–5; Chairman of the Scottish Valuation Advisory Council since 1987, and Trustee of the National Library of Scotland since 1978.

The Rt. Hon. Lord Justice Butler-Sloss DBE was a barrister in the Inner Temple from 1955 to 1970; Registrar Principal, Registry Family Division 1970–79; High Court Judge Family Division 1979–88; Court of Appeal 1988–. She was Chairman of the Cleveland Child Abuse Inquiry 1987–8. She holds honorary degrees from the Universities of Hull, Bristol, Keele, Exeter and Loughborough, and is Hon. Fellow of Kilda's College, Oxford and Presentation Fellow of King's College, London. She is also joint author of various legal textbooks.

The Rt. Hon. Lord Fraser of Carmyllie QC was appointed Minister of State at The Scottish Office on April 14, 1992 with responsibilities for Health, Social Work and Home Affairs, including constitutional matters and all Scottish business in the House of Lords. Prior to his appointment as Minister of State, he was appointed Lord Advocate in 1989 and became a member of the Privy Council the same year. He was a Conservative member of Parliament for South Angus from 1979 to 1983 and Angus East from 1983 to 1987. He was also Solicitor General for Scotland from 1982 until 1989.

Stewart Asquith is St Kentigern Professor for the Study of the Child and Director of the Centre for the Study of the Child and Society at the University of Glasgow. Previously he worked in the Scottish Office and taught at the University of Edinburgh in the Department of Criminology and then later in the Department of Social Policy and Social Work.

Margaret Cox has been Regional Reporter in Grampian Region since 1991. She had previously worked in Strathclyde Reporters' Department in 1982 after four years social work practice and two years experience working for the DHSS. She moved to Grampian in 1989 where she was course leader on the postgraduate Diploma in Social Work.

John Chant CBE is Director of Social Work in Lothian Region and had previously been Director of Social Services in Somerset. He was Social Work Assessor to both the Darren Clark Inquiry in 1978 and the Cleveland Inquiry in 1988 and was Hon. Sec. of the Association of Directors of Social Work from 1982 to 1986.

Alan Finlayson graduated in Arts and in Law at the University of Edinburgh, and was a partner in a solicitor practice until 1970, specialising in criminal and matrimonial law. In 1970 he was appointed Reporter for the then City of Edinburgh on the setting up of the Children's Hearings System and on local government reorganisation was appointed Reporter for Lothian Region. Now retired, he undertakes freelance and consultancy work for the Social Work Services Group and local authorities in the general field of child law. He also sits as Temporary Sheriff.

Kathleen Marshall is Director of the Scottish Child Law Centre, Visiting Professor to the School of Social Work at Queen's College Glasgow, and a Council member of the Children's Rights Development Unit – a new UK-wide charity aiming to promote and monitor implementation of the United Nations Convention on the Rights of the Child. She qualified as a solicitor in 1975 and worked initially in local government in Glasgow. She has been with the Scottish Child Law Centre for four years, during which she has been heavily engaged in considerations for law reform.

INTRODUCTION

STEWART ASQUITH

The Clyde Report *(Report of the Inquiry into the Removal of Children from Orkney in February 1991)* has to be seen in the context of what was a year of considerable activity in the field of child law in Scotland. At the time of the conference in 1992 on which this book is based, a number of reports had already been, or were about to be published. These included the *Report on Family Law* (Scottish Law Commission), the Finlayson Report on *Reporters to the Children's Panel: their Role, Function and Accountability* (Scottish Office), the *Report of the Inquiry into Child Care Policies in Fife* (Kearney Report, Scottish Office) and, published just after the conference, the Skinner Report, *Another Kind of Home: a Review of Residential Child Care* (Scottish Office).

But even before the publication of these reports in 1992, a number of other developments had taken place which will inevitably influence the future of child law and child care in Scotland. In particular, the *Review of Child Care Law in Scotland* (report of a review group appointed by the Secretary of State, chaired by J. W. Sinclair) had been published in 1989 and in December 1991, the United Kingdom ratified the United Nations Convention on the Rights of the Child. The significance of the UN Convention is reflected in the fact that a number of the reports which were to be published after ratification, including those already mentioned above, acknowledged the value of and need to base future developments on the principles of the Convention.

But the Clyde Report also has to be seen in relation to institutions, policies and practices very different from those in existence south of the border in England and Wales. It is undoubtedly the case that, as the contributions to the conference emphasised, many parallels can be drawn between the concerns raised by the Orkney Report and those identified in the Cleveland Report. Nevertheless, the very different educational, social work, child care, juvenile justice and legal systems of Scotland have to be taken into consideration. In particular, the

1

Children's Hearings System, though the Orkney Inquiry did not focus exclusively on it, is an important factor in any attempt to understand both what may have happened in Orkney and also the nature of some of the recommendations made by Lord Clyde.

Nevertheless, both the Clyde Report in Scotland and the Cleveland Report in England and Wales reflect the growing concern with the difficulty of establishing legal and other guidelines for the urgent removal of children from their home in the interests of protecting them from harm while at the same time recognising parental rights and responsibilities; in particular, the opportunity afforded to parents for challenging the validity of the grounds on which a child has been removed from home, has been the focus of specific attention. The relationship between the child's best interests, the rights of the parents and state intervention has been a notoriously difficult one to establish and developments in child protection have largely focused on this. In that respect, both the Cleveland and Clyde Reports make recommendations about the management of child protection cases, premised upon very similar concerns which have their roots in the child abuse inquiries of the seventies and eighties. The different legislative frameworks of the respective jurisdictions should not be allowed to mask the common and wider themes which underpin the developments in child care and child protection in both Scotland, and England and Wales.

CHILD PROTECTION IN A UK CONTEXT

Much of the public and media interest in child care and child protection work has focused largely on the activities of the social work profession. The dilemma for social work in cases of alleged abuse of children, and which surely fuels this public and media interest, is that precipitate intervention is seen as unwarranted and as an invasion of the rights, autonomy and privacy of the family, whereas the failure to intervene in certain cases is also seen as reprehensible because of the dire consequences for the children involved. What has compounded the problem is that in a number of cases where children have suffered and have even died, they have in fact been in care or at the very least known to the authorities. So not only has the timing of intervention by social workers been an issue, but so too have there been questions asked of the judgment and practices of the social work profession. Nowhere is this more obvious than in both the Cleveland and Orkney cases, though the criticisms directed at those who made the decision to intervene there merely echo similar earlier complaints particularly about the social work profession.

From the early seventies onwards, from the death of Maria Colwell and the subsequent inquiry, there has been a clear demand for reform in child care law and practice and it is perhaps a sad comment on developments in child protection that legislative change has usually followed events in which children have been the victims of appalling injuries, resulting often in their death. The cases of Jasmine Beckford and Kimberley Carlile in the eighties added to the demand for reform, and specific recommendations in relation to the law and practices governing the emergency removal of children were made in the reports of the respective inquiries (see Blom-Cooper 1985; 1987).

But public and media concern at the ways in which cases of child abuse were dealt with were also supported by the growing body of research evidence which had presented a very negative image of the quality of care provided to children in care, particularly in relation to the maintenance of contact between children and their families, and the lack of preparation of sound strategies for intervention at a time of crisis in a child's life (see for example DHSS 1985; Packman 1986; Millham et al. 1986).

The research and earlier inquiries of the eighties had identified a number of issues which were to influence policy, practice and legislation and which, nevertheless, were also to be commented on in both the Cleveland and Orkney Inquiries. These included the knowledge base available to inform understanding of child abuse and child sexual abuse; the adequacy of the training afforded to those charged with dealing with such cases; the possibility of early appeal for parents against the decision to remove a child from home; and the need for greater inter-agency cooperation.

CHILD PROTECTION IN SCOTLAND

Although it has been important to trace briefly the themes common to child protection in both Scotland, and England and

Wales, the different legal context for child care in both countries presents a crucial variable in our understanding of the practices and policies developed to deal with child abuse and child sexual abuse. The Children's Hearings System in Scotland offers a very different structure from the more court-based forum of England and Wales for dealing with cases where it is alleged that children have been abused.

The authority for social workers to protect children from abuse and neglect in Scotland is provided by the 1968 Social Work (Scotland) Act, which also introduced the Children's Hearings System. Under the 1968 Act, social work departments are given:

> a statutory duty to cause inquiries to be made and to take action to protect where there is reasonable cause to suspect that a child is suffering or is likely to suffer significant harm . . . the abuse of children as opposed to the actions of adults is defined by the child care legislation rather than the legislation dealing with specific criminal offences against children (Association of Directors of Social Work 1992, para. 1.5.1).

The children's hearings play a central role in determining appropriate measures of care for children who are alleged to have been either physically or sexually abused, with, as in all cases coming before the hearings, the emphasis being on the best interests of the child.

As well as being the year in which the reports referred to earlier in this introduction were published, 1992 was also important for the Scottish Children's Hearings System itself in that it celebrated twenty-one years since its introduction, based on the recommendations of the Kilbrandon Committee on Children and Young Persons (1964). What has been remarkable about the children's hearings and the philosophy of welfare on which it is based is that despite a number of challenges and demands for change, any change that has taken place has been incremental – the fundamental philosophy, structure and operation of the hearings in Scotland has remained relatively unaltered. And though there has been continual questioning, as there has been in other countries, about the merits and efficacy of the system, none of the reports alluded to earlier have made significant criticisms of the basic philosophy of the children's hearings. Nor has the Clyde Report threatened the basic integrity of the Hearings System.

The Hearings System is based on a number of key principles derived from the Kilbrandon Report. In all cases, the welfare of the child is paramount, irrespective of the reasons for which the child is referred to a hearing, whether s/he is in need of care and protection or has committed an offence. Moreover, reflecting the fact that the hearing is not a court of law, there is a clear separation of the decision on matters of fact on the one hand and on the need for compulsory measures of care on the other. The hearings can only decide on the appropriateness of compulsory measures of care and have no punitive options. Parents and children are involved in the discussions at the hearings and parents have a right of appeal to the Sheriff on either the referral or the decision of the hearing.

In all cases, a key role is played by the Reporter to the Children's Panel whose prime function on the basis of information gathered is to make an initial assessment on the need for compulsory measures of care.

The role played by the reporter largely determines the profile of the cases which proceed through the system, since all initial referrals are made to the reporter who will then make an assessment about which cases will proceed to the actual hearings. The discretionary powers exercised by the reporter is reflected in the fact that there is wide variation between the regions of Scotland in the relative proportion of cases which proceed to the hearing stage.

The expectation expressed by the Kilbrandon committee was that the major element in the work of the hearings would be in relation to children referred on offence grounds and in the earlier stages of operation that was certainly the case. But in recent years, there has been a dramatic shift in the proportion of cases referred on care and protection grounds including those cases where children are beyond parental control or have been the victim of an offence.

Between 1980 and 1990, whereas the increase in referrals on offence grounds was around 35%, there was a 155% increase in referrals on care and protection grounds, with a higher proportion of these than of the offence cases actually proceeding to a hearing.* The complexity of the care and protection cases

* SWSG Statistical Bulletin 1992.

means that not only has the volume of cases in this field increased but these are also cases which require considerably more time and involvement of key personnel. Many of the referrals are of course for physical or sexual abuse. What was significant about the Orkney situation and what undoubtedly contributed to the intensity of the public and media interest, was not simply that there were allegations of child sexual abuse but that these were accompanied by claims of ritualistic abuse of a number of children from a number of families in a small island community.

What also has to be remembered about child care in Scotland is that there is an intricate set of relationships between the children's hearings and the courts. For example, as it is not a court of law, a hearing cannot determine the facts of a case if disputed and the case must be referred to the Sheriff to have the grounds established; in the case of appeals against the decision of a hearing, appeals are made to the Sheriff; and there are also a number of clearly specified cases which are dealt with by the Sheriff rather than the hearing.

In relation to child protection cases in particular, whereas the decision about the need for compulsory measures of care, as for all cases referred to the hearings, is the responsibility of the hearing members, Place of Safety Orders can be granted only by the courts or a JP. And, again reflecting the protocol for cases generally, where the facts of a case are disputed, the facts must be established by the Sheriff. Without going into the details of child protection procedures in Scotland, under current law there is a relatively clear separation of the respective responsibilities of the hearings and the courts. Nevertheless, even before the Clyde Report, the adequacy of such procedures as exist for dealing with child protection cases had been questioned, notably in the Child Care Law Review (1989).

CHILD PROTECTION IN ENGLAND AND WALES, AND THE CLEVELAND REPORT

The purpose of the conference on which this book is based was to examine the main findings and recommendations of the Orkney Report in the light of the lessons which may or may not have been learnt from the Cleveland Inquiry.

6

* The Cleveland Report had examined the arrangements for dealing with suspected cases of child sexual abuse in Cleveland in 1987. The Inquiry started in August 1987 and reported in June 1988. The recommendations included:

- Greater recognition and more accurate data on child sexual abuse.
- Taking seriously what the child has to say.
- Taking the views and wishes of the child into account although 'these should not necessarily predominate'.
- Children should not be subjected to repeated medical examinations nor repeated interviewing.
- Parents should be kept informed and where appropriate consulted, receive all important decisions in writing, be advised of rights of appeal, and not left isolated and bewildered.
- Place of Safety Orders should be sought for the minimum time necessary and there should be a code of practice for administration by social workers of emergency orders.
- Structured arrangements for professional supervision and support of social workers.
- Area review committees/joint child abuse committees should review arrangements for training.
- Development of inter-agency cooperation.
- Establishment of specialist assessment teams to undertake full multidisciplinary assessment of child and family.
- Improved training including urgent need for immediate in-service training to professionals to bring them up to date on child sexual abuse.
- Need for inter-agency training.
- Other detailed recommendations covered Place of Safety Orders, Emergency Protection Orders, juvenile courts, guardians *ad litem* and the media.

Most of the recommendations contained in the Cleveland Report have now been implemented throughout England and Wales. Some were the subject of practice guidance issued shortly after the report, whereas others were gathered into the Children Act 1989 or into the associated regulations and guidance.

But at the heart of the Cleveland Report was the concern, identified above, to ensure that there are adequate legal powers

---

* The summary of the Cleveland Recommendations is based on the conference factsheet prepared by Children in Scotland.

to secure the protection of children when emergencies or crises occur but which are open to ready and early appeal and challenge by parents and other interested parties. Excessive and unwarranted use of Place of Safety Orders had been the focus of considerable examination in the Cleveland Report and similar concerns had preoccupied Blom-Cooper (1987). The 1989 Children Act consequently introduced new emergency procedures derived in large part from the recommendations of both these inquiries and in particular provided for two new types of orders – Child Assessment Orders and Emergency Protection Orders.

> The Child Assessment Order is to be sought on the basis of reasonable cause to suspect existing or future harm, the need for an assessment of health, development or the child's treatment to determine whether there is such harm or it is likely in the future and the need for such an order to allow the assessment to take place (Vernon 1990, p. 36).

The Emergency Protection Order is to replace the Place of Safety Order and provides for the removal of the child from home or placement in specific accommodation. And in recognition of the need to acknowledge the interests and rights of parents, the Emergency Protection Order is limited to eight days (with possible extension for another seven days) and application by the child, parents or others may be made to have the order discharged after 72 hours of its being in force.

The merit of highlighting the significance of the new orders in England and Wales is that they are premised upon arguments that were to later reverberate in the Orkney Inquiry and were to provide possible models for future change in Scottish child care policy as proposed by The Scottish Office (Feb 1993).

It would of course be impossible to detail the different sections of the Children Act and its working in this brief introduction. Nevertheless, quite apart from the changes made as regards Place of Safety Orders, the 1989 Children Act is also based on a number of principles which have influenced thinking about child protection in Scotland, mainly because of the common origins of such issues. In particular, the Act identifies the views of children and the need to protect the rights of children as of crucial importance; it emphasises parental responsibility and the importance of contact between families and children; and it also seeks a balance between the child's best interests and the right to autonomy and privacy of parents and the family. The resolution of the delicate relationship between the three key players of the child, the parents and the state at a time of crisis is one that was also inevitably sought by the Clyde Inquiry.

What is apparent from the discussions and contributions to the conference in November 1992 is that the Orkney Report echoes many of the concerns which had been expressed in the earlier report in England. What is also apparent though is the way in which the lessons that were available from the Cleveland Inquiry and from the earlier inquiries in England and Wales, do not appear to have altered practice to any great extent, at least on the evidence presented to us through the medium of the Orkney Report. The report also makes clear the inadequacy of current levels of knowledge and information about child abuse, child sexual abuse and how these are dealt with, particularly in smaller, under-resourced authorities.

BACKGROUND TO THE ORKNEY INQUIRY*

In 1987, a woman on the island of South Ronaldsay in Orkney reported her husband to the police; he was later convicted of physical and sexual abuse of his children and was jailed for seven years.

Three years later, seven children from this family were taken into care because of alleged sibling abuse. While they were in care, the children made disclosures which led social workers to believe that organised sexual abuse was occurring on the island; in particular, they made allegations about the abuse of nine children from four other families, and named the alleged perpetrators. Following an investigation conducted by the Orkney Social Work Department, the RSSPCC, and the police, Place of Safety Orders were obtained from a Sheriff and the nine children were removed from their homes in February 1991.

* This description of background events is derived largely from the conference factsheet prepared by Children in Scotland.

The children were the subject of a referral to the children's hearing, but their parents denied the grounds for referral, and a proof hearing to establish the grounds was arranged before the Sheriff. In April 1991 Sheriff Kelbie held that the proceedings were flawed because of procedural irregularities; the evidence in relation to the alleged abuse was never heard, and the children were returned to their families that same day.

In June 1991, Lord Clyde was appointed by the Secretary of State for Scotland to conduct an inquiry into the actions of the agencies involved in the removal of the nine children. The inquiry's terms of reference specifically excluded any investigation of the original allegations of abuse. The resulting *Report of the Inquiry into the Removal of Children from Orkney in February 1991* was published in October 1992, on the same day as the *Report of the Inquiry into Child Care Policies in Fife*, which examined child care policies in Fife including a number of related issues.

What also has to be remembered is that whether there had ever been group or organised abuse had *never* been established, given the dismissal of the case by Sheriff Kelbie, and that the Orkney Inquiry was essentially about how the whole affair had been managed. The terms of reference of the Orkney Inquiry (1992) were:

> to inquire into the actings of Orkney Island Council (in particular those of their Social Work Department and of their Reporter to the Children's Panel for their area), of the Northern Constabulary and of all persons acting on behalf of either of them, and into the effect of those actings and the attendant publicity in relation to:
>
> 1 the decision to seek authority to take to a place of safety nine children resident in South Ronaldsay
> 2 the removal of those children from their homes on 27th February 1991
> 3 the detention of those children in places of safety following their removal and until returned to their homes (and in particular how they were cared for and interviewed while so detained)
> 4 the decision not to continue proceedings before the Sheriff for a finding on the evidence;
> and to make recommendations (para. 1.3).

THE CLYDE REPORT: MAIN RECOMMENDATIONS*

The main recommendations of the Orkney Report include:

Child Protection

- Child law reform in general, and child protection in particular, should take account of the European Convention on Human Rights and the UN Convention on the Rights of the Child.

- Allegations made by a child regarding sexual abuse should be treated seriously, should not necessarily be accepted as true, but should be thoroughly examined and tested before any action is taken.

- Recommendations on investigation include in relation to multiple sexual abuse, a high level of secrecy and careful planning; designation of senior members of staff of police and social work departments to coordinate joint work; and special arrangements to ensure cooperation between the different agencies involved in separate local authorities.

- Improved coordination of investigations between police and social work, with joint training and joint guidelines as a means of securing this.

- All agencies involved with children should be alert to possible signs of sexual abuse; schools in particular should have close links with social work departments, with training of designated teachers.

- Consideration to Sheriffs having the power to have a suspected abuser excluded from contact with the child.

- Consideration of alternatives to prosecution in appropriate cases, and alternatives to imprisonment at least in cases of intrafamilial abuse.

- Guidelines should not be mandatory but guidance for normal procedure; new national guidance should cover inter-agency liaison and cooperation.

- Establishment of a central resource to provide assistance, particularly to smaller authorities.

- More research into child sexual abuse, and in particular, cases of multiple abuse and provision of personal social services in the islands.

*The summary of recommendations of the Clyde Report is derived largely from the conference factsheet prepared by Children in Scotland.

The Removal of Children to Places of Safety

- 'Child Protection Orders' to empower removal of child where necessary for protection where no alternative exists and where required by 'urgency of the risk'.
- Detailed recommendations relating to the procedures for Child Protection Orders include the orders being obtained where practicable from Sheriffs and not JPs; further training of JPs; qualification of the reporter's existing power to have the child returned by the proviso that the child should not be exposed to the risk of significant harm.
- Recommendations relating to the enforcement of orders and Interim Protection Orders include the welfare of the child remaining the prime consideration in timing the removal of the child; those involved in complex cases being given full, written instructions; social workers and police officers removing children being given sufficient information to enable them to inform the child and parents about the place of safety and a spare copy of the order and explanatory document being left with the parent.

Children in Places of Safety

Detailed recommendations were made covering management, facilities, foster carers, parents, medical examination and interviewing of the children, and included that due consideration be given to the views of the child. A pilot scheme to enhance the role of a 'safeguarder' was suggested before further consideration is given to the possible development of a child's advocate. Extensive detailed recommendations in relation to interviewing included greater recognition of the complexity involved in interviewing children in relation to allegations of sexual abuse; and national guidelines for investigative interviews.

Children's Panel and Reporter

- Consideration of review of the work of children's hearings in the area of child protection, including transfer of all matters relating to a child in a Place of Safety Order to the Sheriff.
- Recommendations in relation to procedure include allowing a parent, guardian or safeguarder immediate recourse to the Sheriff on whether a child requires to be in a place of safety, and entitlement to apply to the Sheriff for recall of the order at any time within seven

days of a child's removal; allowing a child to have an immediate opportunity to have an order varied or cancelled by the Sheriff; transfer of the processing of Child Protection Orders from the children's hearing to the Sheriff; consideration of further restrictions on press reporting of hearings.

· Recommendations on the role of the reporter include recognition of a reporter's independence of action in discussions with social work departments; a reporter considering abandonment of a case passed to the Sheriff for proof, should consult the social work department before action; consideration to preparation of guidance for reporters to secure greater uniformity and practice across Scotland.

Agencies and the Community

· Child protection work should be seen as a specialist area with increased training and support.
· Introduction of a three-year qualifying course for social workers; development of more extensive post-qualifying training to cover interviewing children in cases of suspected sexual abuse; more joint training between social work and other agencies including the police.
· More training for police participation in interviewing children.
· Improved public understanding of child protection; accessibility of social workers to the community and avoidance of technical jargon.

In many respects the Clyde Report repeats the general concerns voiced in the Cleveland and earlier inquiries, and that is perhaps not surprising given their common origins. But on a more negative note, they also reveal the way in which some of the lessons offered by the earlier inquiries have not been taken on board.

A central issue to the Orkney Report was the level and quality of training and experience of key individuals in the whole affair. One of the major recommendations in the report, that social work qualifying training be extended to three years, had initially been ruled out by the government though funding for specialist training of social workers in the islands is to be immediately increased. The inability of the government to find the appropriate monies for extending the training programme for social workers was to come up a number of times during the conference, largely in response to the presentation made by Lord Fraser.

The report also, however, has to be seen in terms of the contribution it makes to the attempt, addressed in Cleveland and the earlier inquiries, to devise child protection procedures which acknowledge the need to balance protecting children's best interests with a recognition of the rights to autonomy and privacy of the parents and the family. Given the high risk decisions which have to be made and will continue to be made in this context, the recommendations contained in the Clyde Report cannot be expected to make the final definitive statement on how best to resolve this particular issue.

CONFERENCE PROCEEDINGS

Lord Clyde identifies four main issues as worthy of particular consideration. The first relates to the whole question of the occasions on which powers should be available to permit removal of children from their home to a place of safety; recognising that removal of a child from home is a traumatic experience and one that should not be undertaken lightly. Given that the abuse the children were alleged to have experienced must have taken place at least some three months before, the children could be said to be at risk but that the risk was not an imminent one. The suggestion is made that a new form of order, similar to the Assessment Order introduced in England though wider and more varied in scope, be sought, with application to be made to the Sheriff.

The second area of concern identified by Lord Clyde concerns the procedure following the execution of the Place of Safety Order and the availability of a mechanism for the immediate review of the order. The Sheriff is seen as the most appropriate person to whom challenges to the execution of a Place of Safety order can be made. Moreover, a vital new element suggested by Lord Clyde is the immediate opportunity afforded to parents to challenge the removal of their children.

The third area, and one which has general implications for the way in which we deal with children, particularly when they are removed from home, is the actual nature of the detention of children in places of safety. In particular, Lord Clyde emphasises the way in which the child may be lost sight of in the midst of all the activity surrounding him/her, with no-one responsible or charged with making sure the child is fully taken into consideration. Though he does not argue at this stage for a child advocate, he does identify the enhanced role that may be given to the safeguarder in the Children's Hearings System.

Finally, turning to social work, Lord Clyde reminds us that, though the Social Work Department came in for considerable criticism as a result of its actions in Orkney, the measures adopted and executed were the result of a joint exercise also involving the police. Nevertheless, fundamental questions are asked about the professional status of social work and about the quality and range of the training afforded to social workers.

Alluding to the criticism that the basis of Lord Clyde's recommendations was very narrow, **Lord Fraser** argues that the Orkney situation provided a very real and stringent test of existing legislation, professional practice, and of public attitude and values – indeed a test for the system as whole. As such, the Clyde Report, he argues, provides the opportunity to examine the way in which the existing child protection provisions of the Social Work (Scotland) Act 1968 cope with the challenges events such as those that took place in Orkney pose.

Nevertheless, there can be no doubt that there will be change in the system and Lord Fraser, following the Clyde Report, indicates a number of areas where change may be most required. These are:

· the legislation relating to the removal of a child from home
· the issue of whether only Sheriffs should be involved when authorising the removal of a child when sexual abuse is involved
· the question of the prompt treatment of cases after removal from home
· the issue of situations where the social work department's knowledge and evidence would not justify removal of a child from home, but where there is sufficient concern to warrant getting access to a child to assess his or her condition.

Both the Orkney and Cleveland Reports are acknowledged by Lord Fraser as important landmarks in the development of policies for child protection.

Referring to what she sees as the depressing and disturbing resemblance between the Orkney Report and the Cleveland Report, **Lord Justice Butler-Sloss** suggests that the Orkney Report could have been described as 'Cleveland Revisited' – such are the resemblances. Though the United Kingdom has signed the UN Convention on the Rights of the Child, the conclusions that have to be drawn from events such as those that featured in Cleveland and Orkney, and elsewhere, is that we fall well below the minimum standards required by the Convention for children. The very nature of their being taken into care has, she argues, to be seen as a form of administrative abuse.

In relation to interviewing, training and the role of the press, Lord Justice Butler-Sloss endorses much of what Lord Clyde had to say, emphasising the need for more sophisticated training for those concerned with and who have a responsibility for children. She ends her contribution with a plea for communication between the different groups and individuals concerned with child care.

As an ex-reporter, **Alan Finlayson's** contribution concentrates on the role of the reporter and the relevance to the Orkney recommendations of his own report on reporters. In particular, whilst acknowledging the major contribution made by them to the development of the system as a whole, a case is made for appropriate training for reporters. The changing nature of the profile of work undertaken by reporters, and the heightened public awareness of their work has rendered the issue of accountability an important one. On a similar theme, **Margaret Cox**, also a reporter, argues that the benefits of the last twenty years should not be lost, that the experience be built upon, and that greater involvement of the Sheriff and the judicial process could fundamentally alter the philosophy and operation of the Hearings System to the detriment of the families involved.

Given the amount of discussion allocated to social work and to the specific question of training, it is no surprise that **John Chant**, Director of Social Work in Lothian Region, expresses disappointment at the resistance of the government to adequately fund qualifying training, especially in view of the recommendation of Lord Clyde to increase training to three years instead of two as at present. Social work practice is committed to working with and on behalf of families, but the Clyde recommendations include only two recommendations relating to working with parents. He calls for a fundamental review, not a piecemeal approach, of child care law in Scotland.

In her contribution, **Kathleen Marshall** concentrates on the rights of children and the ways in which we have failed to follow the principle, provided by the Cleveland Report, of treating the child as a person and not as an object of concern. The recommendation made by Lord Clyde, she argues, that the UN Convention on the Rights of the Child should influence the development of child law in Scotland, must be followed. Moreover, in light of the multiplicity of legislative statements which relate to children, a single all-embracing piece of legislation is required.

Stewart Asquith argues that the enhanced role of the safeguarder as suggested by Lord Clyde is not only unclear but ignores the evidence from earlier research that safeguarders are little used already in the Hearings System. The general issue at stake is the extent to which children's rights can best be protected within a system committed to considering their welfare. Other jurisdictions have established child advocates. These he argues could be introduced into the Children's Hearings System without in any way threatening the integrity of the Kilbrandon philosophy.

The contributions from the key speakers have been presented in full. The question and answer discussions following each formal presentation then develop the arguments.

1

LESSONS FROM THE ORKNEY INQUIRY

Rt. Hon. Lord Clyde

I suspect that there may be some people who may imagine that after a public judicial inquiry the chairman of it is, or at least after the experience has necessarily become, an expert in the whole field with which the inquiry was concerned. Speaking wholly for myself I must disclaim any such expertise. One lesson I at least have learned from the Orkney experience is that the subject of child abuse in general and child sexual abuse in particular is or can be a subject of very considerable complexity in its nature, its cause, its discovery and its treatment. I have also become conscious of the stress which the work of investigating child sexual abuse can create in those engaged in it with a consequent risk of intemperate and ill-considered action. I have also become aware of the need for greater public understanding of the problem. Those are some of the lessons which I have learned from Orkney. But I believe there can be advantages in having an outsider look at a particular area of specialist expertise and that there may be benefits in having a member of one profession examining the actings and practices of another. The little girl who identified the truth about the Emperor's new clothes represents the refreshing reality that an innocent bystander may identify curiosities and deficiences which those who are too close to a problem or are too immersed in professional practice may not observe or may not wish to observe.

The matter which required to be investigated in Orkney was of course a somewhat special one. In the first place the question whether there ever had been an incident of group or organised abuse, as certain of the police and social workers believed, had not been established. Nor was it part of the remit which controlled the scope of the investigation which I was asked to carry out. Then again the social and geographical environment, while not unique in every respect, was nevertheless special. This was a relatively isolated island community with its own distinct character and although all of the families most closely concerned were incomers, they formed a part of that community. Further, the allegations were made regarding some nine children of four distinct families. In the next place the allegations that the children in question had been abused had come not from those children themselves but from other children who were already in the care of the local authority and indeed were members of a family with which the social work department had had some concern for a few years. Finally, the removal of the children and the subsequent procedures attracted a quite unusual interest in the media, with an intensity of attention far beyond what had been anticipated.

But while all these features combined to make the case somewhat special, the principles governing the action which was taken remained general. While the special facts gave rise to special problems, the ground rules for investigation, the principles governing the interviewing of children, the main guidelines for the taking of action to protect children in danger were still relevant. Despite the unusual story which lay behind the inquiry the opportunity was I think a reasonable one for studying the generality of the problem in Scotland. Conversely it would, I think, have been unfortunate not to take advantage of the opportunity to review the legal position and the matters of practice involved in the particular case. The observation has been made that it would be wrong to change the law simply because in one highly special case things seem to have gone wrong. But on the other hand, if there are aspects of the law which appear to be less than fair wherever they are applied, then it is proper to propose reform even if it is an unusual case which has drawn attention to them. It is no doubt perfectly true that in countless cases, Place of Safety Orders are sought, granted and enforced without complaint and for the necessary protection of a child. But if the system does not cater adequately or fairly for the occasional case where challenge is made or the removal is open to question then the existence of the many unchallenged cases should not be allowed to stand in the way of reform or to hinder debate on the procedures and practices which should be adopted.

It is tempting to sit down at this stage with the suggestion that so far as I am concerned the lessons from Orkney are set out in the report which has been published and leave it at that. But I am conscious of its relative length and I have a considerable sympathy for anyone who has sought to read the thing from beginning to end. So with an apology to those who have done just that I propose to select four areas of subject matter where some of the principal lessons can be found. To be selective is necessarily dangerous. I may well be taken to be emphasising some matters at the expense of others. But in the interests of time if not also of motion I think that a sample is the proper course. I should also explain that I have looked rather to areas where there is material for recommendation than concentrated on criticisms of what was or was not done in the particular case. Retrospection can be profitable if the study leads to positive future improvement and without that purpose criticism may well prove a barren exercise.

One area for instruction is that of the occasion on which power should be available to remove a child to a place of safety. It should not be necessary to observe that the removal of a child at least from a familiar environment is not a step to be taken lightly, or inadvisedly, in the interest of the child. It will be a traumatic step for the child. Of course the trauma will be absolutely justified where the alternative is the certain exposure to harm. Where injury is imminent then the disturbance and distress involved in a rescue operation are acceptable. But a number of considerations here arise. The first and perhaps the most important concerns the statutory provision in section 37(2) of the Social Work (Scotland) Act 1968.

In practice it has been recognised that this is a provision to be used in cases of emergency. But that is not evident from the Act. It has been reflected in the understanding that Place of Safety Orders should lapse if not enforced within a particular time-limit. But the temptation is there to see them as warrants which can be obtained in case they may be required, when it is not known for certain whether a danger does exist. In the Orkney case about a fortnight elapsed between the decision to seek the orders and the enforcement of them. The evidence of abuse related to an alleged incident which at best must have occurred more than three months before. While in a sense it could be thought that the children were at risk, it is hard to see that the risk was an imminent one.

Where a child is about to be the victim of an attack, or where a child is found to be neglected with no one capable of looking after the child and immediate steps are necessary for the safety of the child, then the removal may be justified. But there may be other cases where the removal under the statutory provision may be questionable or mistaken. The Orkney case provides an example. The problem then is to preserve the operation of the power in the many cases where the action is justified but refine its application so as to avoid misuse. It should be possible to achieve some redirection of the statutory provision towards the kinds of case where it is appropriate that the power should be granted and exercised.

Of course there is no absolute solution to the problem which will with certainty obviate any possible mistake. The most carefully framed legislation cannot be expected to remove all risk of error. Eventually one is brought back to the exercise of discretion and of a professional judgement. More then is needed than a rewriting of the statute. Some guidance should be possible upon the occasions on which the discretion should be exercised. Such guidance should include provision emphasising the need for clear evidence to justify the operation of the provision and the keeping of written records of the grounds of the application and of the grant. At the very least the need to prepare such records can help to concentrate the minds of those involved on the clear necessity for the step which is being contemplated.

Consideration must be given too to the possibility of finding alternatives to the extreme course of removal. If the matter is still at the stage of investigation there may be circumstances where any questioning of the children can be at least deferred. Why should not the concentration be turned on the questioning of adults in the first instance? And if there is reason to suspect that a child is in danger is it necessary to remove the child, or can the situation be alleviated by removal of an adult? The matter is of course one where the circumstances may altogether prevent any alternative course being open beyond the removal of the child. But in every case consideration at least should be given to the existence of possible alternative courses of action.

It is in this context that the suggestion has been made that a new power should be available comparable in some respects with the Assessment Order recently introduced in England but of a much wider and more varied scope. The suggestion is that it should be possible to apply to the Sheriff for an order tailored

22

to the particular neeeds of the particular situation. Thus if the parents were not co-operating but there was serious concern that the child was at risk and it was desired to have the child examined or asked about the matter an order could be obtained to enable that to be done. Again by such an order one adult could be removed from the home if that would remove the risk to the child and still enable the child to remain. Such a power might well prove to be a useful aid to strengthen the work of investigation and avoid the necessity of resort to the extreme course of removal.

The second of the four areas concerns the procedure following execution of a Place of Safety Order and the opportunity for immediate review of it. Despite the restraints and the guidance and the provision of alternatives, it will still be possible for an erroneous view to be formed in perfectly good faith and a child removed in circumstances where the child could with sufficient safety be left at home. Safeguards will always be required. One such safeguard which is pointed to is the Sheriff or JP to whom the application for the order is made. But the court is very substantially dependent upon the person who comes applying for the order to set out the information relevant to the problem so that a balanced and objective view can be formed about it. It may well be quite unrealistic to regard the obtaining of the order on an *ex parte* statement as an examination of the merits of the application for removal, far less as a step which shifts the burden of responsibity for the course from the applicant to the court. Something of a parallel may be found in the application for an interim interdict in the ordinary court. The responsibility for the raising of problems may more regularly there be recognised through the duty which counsel or solicitor owes to the court in the performance of his or her professional responsiblilities, but even then the responsibility for obtaining the order is left firmly on the party applying for it.

The reporter provides one safeguard under the existing statutory scheme since it lies with him in effect to require the child to be returned if he considers that the child does not require compulsory measures of care. But that is a relatively high standard. The case has to be one where it is not even worth taking the matter to a children's hearing. Furthermore it is not a standard which necessarily takes full account of the neccessity for the removal at the current stage of proceedings.

There are also considerations of the rights of the parent and the child which suggest that an immediate means of recourse should be available on the initiative of the child or the parent or guardian whereby the necessity for the removal of the child may be immediately challenged. Once that is recognised in principle the question arises where that recourse should be. Some may argue that the panel should have that function. It might be thought that something of that kind was once envisaged by the legislation, where it required the case of a child taken to a place of safety to be put before a children's hearing wherever practicable not later than the first lawful day after the child has been detained in a place of safety. But that is not how the provision has worked out in practice. The dispute about the first lawful day hearing will be too familiar to rehearse here. There have developed two schools of thought about its function and purpose, and allied with that has been a dispute about what the practicalities are which may properly entitle the reporter to delay holding the hearing. That ambiguity and that dispute certainly requires resolution. On one view of the section, the view which was adopted by the reporter in the Orkney case following practice adopted by many others, a week may pass before the removal of the child comes under challenge and that does not seem acceptable.

It is suggested that the proper person to whom recourse should be had for an immediate challenge to the execution of an order is the Sheriff. It is not unreasonable that the court who granted the order should be asked to reverse it and even if it was granted by a JP or even another Sheriff, it may well be thought more appropriate that the order should be overturned by a court rather than the panel.

There is however a more fundamental reason for suggesting that the Sheriff rather than the hearing should interfere with the order. The jurisdiction of the hearing is essentially in the disposal of the case as distinct from the merits of it, that is the ascertainment of the facts on which the case was raised in the first place. The investigation of the merits has all along been reserved to the Sheriff, so that if the referral is challenged, the hearing is bound to pass the case to the Sheriff to resolve, and it is only if after exploring the facts the Sheriff holds the grounds of the referral to be established that the case returns to the hearing for further disposal. Of course that basic distinction is not absolutely hard and fast. There are repects in which the hearing will at least take note of the facts. But in essence the basic philosophy of the system recognises the distinction of function. It is consistent with that basic distinction that the Sheriff should determine the necessity for the immediate detention of the child. The reality or otherwise of the risk, the strength of the applicant's case and the probability of the grounds being established are matters where the Sheriff's expertise is appropriate.

From there it is a short step to providing that the next question in the case be asked by the Sheriff rather than by the hearing – that is whether the grounds of referral are admitted or not. If they are not, the case is already there in the Sheriff Court and arrangements can be made for the necessary proof in that court to establish the grounds. On the other hand if the grounds are admitted then the Sheriff's participation can terminate and the case be entrusted to the hearing for the subsequent considerations regarding disposal. It should be noted that no major invasion of the jurisdiction of the hearing is being proposed here but merely the retention of the case within the jurisdiction of the Sheriff to allow for the opportunity of a speedy challenge to his order. In the vast majority of cases the grounds will be admitted. The practical result of the change would be that a hearing would not require to convene to hear the grounds admitted or denied. The vital new element is the provision of an immediate opportunity for the parents to challenge the removal of their children.

A third area where there are lessons to be learnt is that of the detention of children in places of safety. There seems to be some doubt as to the precise powers, rights and duties of those involved with the child. The status of a child in the actual custody but not the legal care of the child clearly requires clarification. Once the obligations and powers of the local authority on the one hand and of the parents on the other are sorted out then many of the other problems can be more readily resolved. Thus the problems of communication, of access, of the separation of siblings, and of the personal possessions which the child may retain or have forwarded, and of the securing of his or her continued education can be more easily determined after the legal position has been resolved, and the problems can be approached against the background of a clear understanding of the respective parties' rights and obligations. Where consents are required for examination or interview, the legal background should also be clearly understood.

One real risk which has been voiced is that in the middle of all the energetic activity designed for the benefit of the child, the child may remain isolated and to a degree neglected. Committees may be sitting, minutes may be being taken, case notes being built up, but the object of the whole exercise may be left alone with little understanding of what is going on and with no one to whom he or she can turn for advice or who can take up on a direct and personal basis the needs and interests of the child. The suggested solution is the appointment of someone who would take on that general brief, who could always have direct access to the child and be accessible to the child, and who could speak for the child and represent the child whenever necessary. What is suggested here is not or not yet a child's advocate, but an enhancement of the role of the safeguarder. In many cases such a development may well be unnecessary, but in the more complex cases that service ought to be very much in the consciousness of those engaged in the matter so that if there is any risk of the child being isolated an appointment may be made by the court to reduce that risk. In Orkney, the co-ordinators worked with some energy to protect the children's interests but in one area the uncertainty about her role and status diminished her effectiveness.

One particular area of work which has attracted a measure of publicity and which must be noted in this context is that of the interviewing of children. While it is not too difficult to point out mistakes which can be or have been made it is far more difficult to attempt to set out a complete or comprehensive guide to the art of interviewing children. It is clear that the work of talking with children in the course of an investigation into alleged child abuse is a highly specialised art. The art is far more than a mere matter of knowing what techniques to use or to avoid, but calls for a thorough preparation of the approach to be adopted and a full understanding of the intelligence and development of young people. It is not just a matter of not using leading questions, and even that may not be an absolute rule anyway, but a matter of careful and conscious planning, of knowing exactly what is to be asked and why. There are a number of other questions raised with regard to the interviewing of children, such as the number of times that a child should be interviewed in an investigation, the regularity of the interviews and the identity of the interviewer, but once the true nature of the art is recognised then the other issues of timing and intensity and the rest will fall into place.

The need to keep full records and such things as the labelling of drawings for future reference also require to be noticed. One other aspect which was touched upon may deserve some particular emphasis. That is the necessity for a clear understanding of the ownership of any records which have been made and of the steps to be taken to control the safe custody of those records. The risk of audio or video tapes of interviews escaping into the hands of those who may wish to copy them and make a commercial use out of them is one which has been recognised. The safeguarding of such tapes is a problem which may well deserve careful consideration.

The final chapter of these lessons which I should wish to identify is that which relates to the profession of social work. It is always useful for a profession from time to time to turn and have a hard look at itself, to see how far it is meeting the needs of the present time, whether it requires to reappraise its functions and purposes, whether it is suitably structured, manned and organised to cope with the demands made of it. This is all the more so in the case of a relatively young profession such as that of the social worker. The work of the profession has developed both in volume and variety over the past years. The Younghusband Report and the later establishment of CCETSW have been milestones in the development of the profession. But it may be that the time has come again for a further review of the profession and its role for the next period of its history.

It may well be thought that one essence of a profession is the degree of autonomy which it ought to enjoy. That may involve the setting of its own standards of expertise and qualification, its own decision as to the formal qualifications from educational establishments which it will recognise, the setting of its own standards of what is and what is not acceptable professional conduct. Professional bodies usually have their own disciplinary bodies and their own disciplinary procedures. They can receive complaints and can investigate the conduct of their members. Has the time come when the social work profession should start developing itself as a profession in the true sense?

One feature of the Orkney case which is common with many other cases was the readiness with which criticism was focused on the social workers to the almost entire exclusion of the police. Yet the whole operation of the removal of the children was a joint exercise planned and executed by both of those agencies. The phenomenon can be explained in terms of the ancient standing of the one agency compared with the other and the public perception of the essential nature of the police function for the maintenance of law, order and civilised behaviour in society. It certainly seems to be the case that the police force is able to withstand the occasional human failing which may occur within any organisation more robustly than can the profession of social worker. A better understanding of the role and the achievements of the social work profession might help but above all what seems to be required is the kind of increase in status and respect which a higher level of training and membership of a skilled profession might inspire. The need for joint training, especially with the police, and close coordination with the police in the investigation of child abuse is also an area for consideration.

The suggestion of a three-year training period was of course no novel suggestion nor is there anything new in the immediate reaction which it has received. But what is to happen next? If there did exist a formally constituted professional body even for Scotland I wonder whether the problem might not be tackled by some independent initiative from within the profession. There are professional bodies who secure or even organise their own training programmes. Are there no original sources for funding which might be tapped? Are there no initiatives which the profession could devise within itself to secure the results which it sees as desirable or even necessary for the enhancement of the profession?

Beyond all of that, thought may have to be given to the public image and reputation of the profession, and the necessity for demonstrating that what may too often pass as the popular image is not the reality, or to the extent that it does represent something of a reality, to secure that the appropriate changes are made. It may be that the profession starts from a disadvantage in the fact that to a large extent it may be seen as an arm of the local authority and so viewed as an authoritarian body which is there to exercise statutory powers over the citizen in accordance with statutory procedures. As the Orkney experience showed, the profession calls for qualities of a high order, not only humanity and humility but a sensitive expertise and a sound common sense, a very considerable patience and the courage to meet with and talk to people whose hostility may seem to frustrate any communication. Many members of the profession of course display these qualities and thereby can give the lie to the popular misconception. The more they can be demonstrated the more readily can the public image be enhanced. Even the development of the art of simple communication and the avoidance of professional jargon is something to be considered. The development of specialisations and the examination of the suitability of particular individuals to embark on particular areas of work may deserve thought.

Of course the inquiry did not explore in depth the whole range of the profession's work even in Orkney. The matter of the future of the profession is one for further study and I would hope for further public debate. It may be that this Society (*Children in Scotland*) is a forum for that discussion to be developed. Certainly I am grateful to it for organising this gathering to pursue further the various matters to which the Orkney Inquiry may have given rise, only some of which I have touched upon. As will have been noted by those who have managed to read the report, many of the recommendations relate to questions which may deserve further debate. I am glad to be present at what I hope may be the start of a period of constructive discussion which may in turn lead to reform and improvement of a service which is as vital to the community as it is not appreciated, and as deserving of admiration as it is so often misunderstood.

DISCUSSION

David Bowie
Assistant District Manager, Strathclyde Social Work Department

'I would like to ask Lord Clyde to elaborate a little further on the functioning as he sees it, of the Interim Protection Orders. That seems to me to be a very important part of the recommendations.'

LORD CLYDE

'The best way I think I can answer that question is in a fairly general way, because the object of the exercise, or the object of the idea, was to provide as flexible and as wide a power as could be conceived. It is very difficult always to anticipate all the things that may be required in particular cases, and I would be reluctant if the framers of whatever comes out of that idea restricted it too much to specific powers so as to confine its scope and prevent it being used in some strange circumstance which, no doubt, will turn up within a year of the legislation being passed, and not be covered by it. The inspiration of course was partly from England, but we did note that the English power appeared to be designed for certain particular purposes which, if I recall correctly, were set out in the legislation. We were anxious to try and leave the matter as open as possible and enable the power to be used not only for enabling an investigation to be made – for children to be taken for a day, or even if necessary overnight, for a medical examination or interview in circumstances where the family is not cooperating and refuses to let the child be released, or something of that kind – but also, to enable other things to be done, such as the temporary removal of an adult from the household, where there was perhaps another adult who was perfectly safe or regarded as safe and could still look after the child, and not expose the child to the experience of removal unneccessarily. I would be anxious, and I think this is the best way I can answer the question, to see powers as general as possible so that it can cover future unanticipated contingencies.'

Detective Chief Inspector Holden
Central Scotland Police

'I was wondering if I could draw Lord Clyde perhaps a bit more on the subject of joint training for police and social workers.

I know as a practitioner in the field, and with my colleagues in the Central Region Social Work Department, that we feel strongly that joint training is very important. Some of the guidelines we have are very vague, in fact there are no guidelines in regard to length or residential content. I note that you said child development and child behaviour is a very important part of training and I wondered if the description that it is an area for consideration is strong enough. I wondered if I could draw you on that.'

LORD CLYDE

'Now it's moments like this, you see, that one really gets the truth about the first paragraph of what I said, because you are expecting someone who is professedly not an expert in this field to give views which will almost certainly be subject to criticism by those who know far more about it. I was certainly impressed by the recognition, I think by everybody who was covering that area of the matter, of the desirability or necessity for joint training to be done, and perhaps the first hurdle is to overcome the difficulty there might be in accepting that two fairly distinct agencies should be cooperating to that extent. I think probably the next step might be, once that philosophy can be established, that certainly in the area of child protection, and there may well be others, joint training is in principle something to be pursued. The next step should be for those who are experts in the field to draw up a short list of particular subjects, more precise subjects which should be the matter for such training courses. Some knowledge of the problems of interviewing children is one; some understanding, possibly some fairly detailed understanding of the whole problem of child abuse – something of how it comes about, something about its prevalence and certainly something about the indicators that may be picked up by people who come into contact with children – something about the whole of their background understanding. Those are two fairly obvious examples. And then the practice of dealing with the problem – it would be certainly useful, I would have thought, for both agencies to have a clear understanding of the parts to be played by respective members and respective agencies. But I would be very happy if somebody deeply knowledgeable about this area would give the appropriate answer to it. But those are at least some suggestions.'

Susan Davidson
Staff Development Officer, Barnardo's

'Lord Clyde, you mentioned the need for a specialised skill in terms of staff talking to children. Do you have any comments about the skill required of senior managers in maybe managing this kind of situation?'

LORD CLYDE

'I speak in generalities here. Quite certainly I would have thought that senior managers must have that skill in some contexts. It may be appropriate in a complex case to have the senior management's participation quite extensively. They may be required to be keeping more of a monitoring and supervision responsibility in the course of the interviews themselves and I would certainly hope that at that level, it was not a matter, certainly in complex cases, to be left to the lower levels themselves to carry on without a close eye being kept upon it.'

Kathleen Marshall
Scottish Child Law Centre

'You mentioned the possibility of excluding a suspected abuser and you related this to the granting of an Interim Protection Order, and I wondered whether you have considered having that as a power in relation to the Child Protection Order as such, which would possibly last for a longer period. Was it meant to be limited to the Interim Protection Order?'

LORD CLYDE

'Yes. One doesn't want to get tied up with too much in the way of technical terms here. What I would be looking for is provision which would enable that power to be used in any circumstances at all, so that it would not just be seen as a stage necessary which you had passed when anything else happened. One could remove the child, then remove the adult and put the child back for example, so if that was your concern, that one might have passed that hurdle, and then no longer be able to have access to it, or passed that opportunity then not have access to it, that wasn't what was looked for. It would be something to be there in the background all along. There was, I think, some discussion and I cannot, I confess, remember from which source it came – I would probably be doing somebody an injustice, I hope it wasn't yourself – in relation to this particular matter as to the stage at which this power might be available. But again, I think in all of this, one wants to be looking for the greatest flexibility so that the powers are there to be used in the interests of the child whatever the particular circumstances may be.'

Angela Harte
Lothian Region Social Work Department

'Just to actually continue that point on further, would you see that as actually being useful in treatment, because that is often the stumbling block for us with children, as to actually have access to them, to work with them once the investigation is all over.'

LORD CLYDE

'I hadn't put in it that way. There were limits to the remit in Orkney and the whole area of treatment was one which we didn't embark on at all, but I can see the force of what you say and that again is probably a further example of desirability of framing the thing. I do recall that one of the many distinguished contributors on the expert side to the inquiry did question whether this kind of interim power with the assessment order idea was necessary at all, but I think the point was accepted (at least I hope it has been) that it is only a power and there may be advantages in having it in particular circumstances. It should do no harm to have it. It could be a valuable weapon in particular cases which just require that extra assistance.'

Alex Hamilton
Grampian Region Social Work Department

'Not directly related to your contribution this morning, Lord Clyde, but one which is touched upon I think somewhat paradoxically in the report, is the issue about believing children, which very clearly also needs to go into the equation of the knowledge, the skills and the information that is coming to people when they are grappling with these very difficult issues. I wonder if you might make comment on that please.'

LORD CLYDE

'I am sorry if it was paradoxical! I doubt that there is very much more that I can usefully reformulate beyond what I tried to say. One has to be so careful in so much of this not to be carried away by little mottos like: 'the child is to be believed'. It is absolutely sound, I am sure, to recognise that there may be, or have been in the past, assumptions about how far or whether what a child says is to be accepted, or what level of respect what a child says is to receive. These are of course useful expressions in facing up to the particular problem, but there can never be an absolute. It would be quite wrong, I would have thought, to say in every circumstance, a child is to be believed. One must always preserve in one's mind the possibility that the child is mistaken and whilst one must certainly respect what the child says and not come with some predisposition that 'oh it's a child therefore it can't be right', or that 'what a child says requires something of less respect that what an adult says'. Nevertheless, it is again the catchphrase – 'the open mind' – that has to be preserved there and I think one has simply to be looking carefully without prejudice, impartially, objectively and making the assessment in each particular case without any clear, certainly no preconceptions but with very little guidance in what is a very difficult field.'

Neil Watson
District Officer, Child Care, Strathclyde

'One of the major traumas for children in these situations aside from the removal into care can be the interface with the legal process and the adversarial nature of the legal process. If you are recommending that the challenge to an Interim Protection Order or a Place of Safety Order is done again within a legal situation, in front of a Sheriff, how do we avoid that becoming yet one more traumatic experience for children, where solicitors or whoever can badger them, and the adversarial nature of that particular case would cause a traumatic effect on children?'

LORD CLYDE

'Because the Sheriff has a much greater power, and with all respect to the Hearings, sometimes an even greater ability to keep members of the legal profession in order, it is very difficult and understandably difficult sometimes for some lay tribunals to control high powered members of the legal profession. You are actually right of course in expressing the concern but I would have thought that in a private hearing in a Sheriff's chambers with the degree of informality which can be achieved there and the control of a Sheriff, those dangers should be minimised than might be the case in another forum.'

2

LEGISLATING FOR CHILD PROTECTION

RT. HON. LORD FRASER OF CARMYLLIE

I am glad to have the opportunity to address this conference and to contribute to this discussion of child protection. It is a privilege to be associated with two distinguished speakers today – Lord Justice Butler-Sloss and Lord Clyde – both of whom have produced reports which have such wide and important implications for the protection of children.

This is a major topic of public concern and one which provokes all kinds of reactions and raises all kinds of emotions. This is a complex area in which it is never wise to rush to judgements. Lord Clyde's report provides an excellent model of the careful consideration and wise judgements that must be brought to bear. For professional staff involved – particularly social workers – child protection is testing and often stressful. In looking to future legislation we need to be clear-thinking and to consider the practical implications of changes in a wide range of situations. We need to show true commitment to all children in society; we must see child protection as the protection of our children from harm. One of their most important rights is to have all decisions about them made with care and we have that very clearly in mind as we prepare our White Paper on Child Care Policy and Law for Scotland.

But before going into my given subject, I would like to offer a caveat. It would be wrong to give the impression that child protection has somehow or other an existence of its own – with its own rationale, its own way of dealing with children and calling for its own skills. Child protection is part, but only a part, of child care as a whole. This care embraces a variety of services, from providing support to families and children in order to prevent stress and problems, through to providing residential care for some of the most disturbed and difficult children in a setting where they can have time and space for rehabilitation. Protecting children is part of this range of service, whether it arises in an emergency or through chronic abuse, or because of failure to thrive through prolonged inadequate care. In discharging their duty to protect children in emergencies or otherwise and in working with other services like the police, health and education, social workers should keep good child care practice uppermost in their mind. The best interests of the child should drive every decision and every action.

The title of my address focuses on legislation for protection. As a lawyer, you would expect me to say that the legal arrangements are absolutely crucial – they provide the essential framework of rights, powers and responsibilities within which standards of child care are defined in accordance with what society wants.

But the law – by which I mean both primary legislation and detailed regulations made under it – is not and cannot be the whole story. The law is important but the way in which child protection is judged publicly is very much a reflection of how it is put into practice. The practical problems of child protection show how much more is needed – skills, knowledge, sensitivity and good judgement of all those charged with providing care and protection. Good protection work depends on the quality of practitioners and managers, and the quality of their practice depends on the guidance which helps them to focus on solutions to problems which they find, on the training and knowledge which give them the basic tools which they can deploy in dealing with what are often complex and distressing human situations and finally on the clarity and security of the law within which they act.

As Lord Justice Butler-Sloss knows only too well, the major legislative reform which was introduced in England and Wales through the Children Act 1989 required it to be followed-up not only by detailed regulations, but by guidance and a substantial commitment to training. Clearly we should take careful note of that experience in looking to the reform of child care legislation in Scotland.

We have before us now several reports which are of major significance for child care in Scotland in the future.

· The Child Care Law Review published in 1990 as the result of careful consideration by an expert group.
· The Report on the Role and Functions of the Reporter to the Children's Panel produced by an experienced former reporter and now the subject of consultation.

· The Report of Sheriff Kearney's Fife Inquiry into child care policies in one local authority.
· The Report of Lord Clyde's Orkney Inquiry into particular events in another authority.

We hope to have the report of the Review of Residential Child Care in Scotland very shortly.* These various reports and the responses they elicit from agencies in Scotland will be invaluable to us in drawing up proposals for the future in a White Paper on Child Care Policy and Law which we hope to produce in the early part of next year.

In preparation for that part of the White Paper which will deal with child protection, we propose to issue a consultation paper shortly on our thoughts for reforming legislation in Scotland for the future. In doing so, we shall certainly make positive use of Lord Clyde's report which is not only a very thorough analysis of what actually happened when the nine children were removed from South Ronaldsay, but contains thoughtful and helpful proposals for change in the future, encompassing legislation, guidance and training related to child protection.

It has been said that the basis of Lord Clyde's recommendations is very narrow. 'Orkney is not Scotland' we are told. This may be true in one sense but not in another. It would be short-sighted to see events in Orkney as 'a little local difficulty' since they happened in a remote island community under circumstances which seemed unlikely to be replicated anywhere else in Scotland in the near future. The Orkney situation provided a very stringent test of existing legislation, of professional practice and of public attitude and values. It would be complacent to play that test down. Any system must be able to cope with difficult and unusual situations. Orkney was a test of the whole system. It seems to me that it is only right that we should be constantly aware of the developments which occur within child protection, reflecting wider changes in society. We should be prepared to learn lessons – wherever they emerge – and be prepared to respond to them positively. No doubt the events in Orkney brought together a whole

*Published December 1992.

variety of circumstances and created problems in an unusual concentration. The combination of problems would have tested any authority: the impact was all the greater and more visible and dramatic in a small rural island authority with a very small social work department. But it was a test which we cannot ignore. If we were to attempt to do so we would be ignoring the lessons of experience and we would be ignoring Lord Clyde's advice. To quote his own words, he was concerned 'to establish the facts relative to the remit for future benefit rather than past recrimination'.

Lord Clyde has done a great service by prompting us to re-examine some challenging questions underlying the existing child protection provisions of the Social Work (Scotland) Act 1968. He prompts us to re-examine just where the balance lies between providing for the welfare of the child and ensuring that a child and parents enjoy justice in the handling and disposal of child protection cases. In providing for the welfare of children, is our legislation sufficiently sensitive to the issues of justice for children and their families? Is our existing system of checks and balances still right?

The Scottish system has been described by some as a welfare system rather than a justice system. But these are quite false distinctions. Welfare without justice is ultimately no welfare and indeed justice without welfare is scant justice. The system must be a careful intertwining of justice and welfare at every stage. It must be designed to provide the best justice and the best welfare and to prevent either one jeopardising the other. We must 'go for gold' in both.

Lord Clyde's report has many recommendations about legislation but it goes beyond that. If we are to plan ahead with clarity and purpose for future legislation we are bound to look at the essence of his recommendations for changes in the whole field of child protection. We have to recognise that that is very much focused on emergency protection and although he deals to a large extent with legislation, he also deals with more detailed matters which are better suited to regulation and indeed also to guidance, which is strictly speaking beyond the bounds of legislation though complementary to it. In planning change we are bound to aim at a balance of legal prescription and practice guidance.

In the remaining part of my address, I propose to deal principally with what seems to me to be the major aspects of change which should be considered for reform of our legislation, but I also want to say something about the other changes which are complementary to such changes. First, what legislative changes do we have under consideration?

Local authorities can discharge their basic welfare duty to protect children from harm in any of a number of ways. They may take preventative action designed to solve problems without resort to intervention. Or they may persuade a suspected abuser to remove himself voluntarily from the family home. Or they can refer cases to the reporter so that he can consider whether children need compulsory measures of care. In particular circumstances, they may seek authority to remove children immediately from home in order to protect them from harm. It is the last of these modes of approach which inevitably attracts closest public attention. It involves abrupt intervention in the lives of children and their families and it inevitably impinges on the rights and responsibilities of parents. The legal provisions which sanction powers to remove children from home must therefore rest on a careful balance between the child's protection and the parents' responsibilities for the child and the rights which the parents need to have to exercise those responsibilities. But the law is bound to be founded on recognition and interests of the child first and foremost.

Lord Clyde made no fewer than 194 recommendations, many of them related to legislation. From these recommendations I see five main issues calling for new legislation.

First, Lord Clyde recommends that we have to clarify the legal standards which have to be satisfied for removal of a child from home. He suggests that they should be:

1. The child is likely to suffer imminent harm.
2. Harm should be significant.
3. Removal is necessary to secure the child's protection.

This is a standard embodying three important tests. It is far more explicit than the existing power in section 37 of the Social Work (Scotland) Act which does no more than imply a need for emergency action and simply states five types of case in which a child may be considered for removal to a place of safety. It allows for removal on the basis of suspicion and uncertainty, which gives wide scope for discretion. The lack of definition in the scope of the power may well run counter, Lord Clyde suggests, to international conventions. We accept that section 37 requires revision.

Secondly, Lord Clyde recommends greater clarity on the degree of justification for an order to remove a child and that has to be emphasised. The applicant for such an order is in the crucial position of initiating significant action in the life of a family. He or she must provide sufficient information to persuade a Sheriff or JP and this must be examined carefully. We accept this argument. The responsibility for finding even a *prima facie* case for removal is substantial. So much so that Lord Clyde suggests that only Sheriffs should be involved when authorising removal of a child where sexual abuse is involved. There do seem to be some issues here which need detailed consideration. It seems doubtful whether Sheriffs by themselves could reasonably be expected to handle the future traffic of orders. There are practical problems of availability. Either all JPs should be capable of authorising orders or else a significant number of them should be selected and trained to do so. I doubt if it would be practical to steer all sexual abuse cases to Sheriffs. It may be questionable to separate out sexual abuse from other forms of abuse. In practice, there is often overlap between different forms of abuse.

Thirdly, there is the question of prompt treatment of cases after a child has been removed. Here, Lord Clyde has attempted to move delicately into the area of relationships between the Sheriff Court on the one hand and on the other, reporters and children's hearings. He has suggested that a major change should be made to concentrate on the Sheriff consideration of the need for detention, and on the children's hearings assessment of grounds for referral and the measures which – if grounds are agreed or found proved – are in the best interests of the child. The Secretary of State has indicated that he accepts the broad thrust of Lord Clyde's recommendations. The detailed proposals will take into account our forthcoming consultation paper on emergency protection.

Removal of a child from home poses two quite distinct issues – the need for continued detention and the need for measures of care in the interests of the child. The existing legislation allows for appeals to the Sheriff at various stages but the hearing is involved with both questions. What Lord Clyde has suggested seems to be a helpful separation of the two functions, which has the advantage of allowing parents and children to have more or less immediate access to appeals against an order authorising the removal of the child. In that case they would no longer have to await a children's hearing at which grounds for referral may or may not be presented to them. This seems a significant and justified move towards affording more rights to children and parents, in the spirit of the United Nations Convention on the Rights of the Child. Some people might be displeased to see the change as indicating a major reduction of the role of the children's hearings. I do not accept this. The net effect would be to concentrate the children's hearings on what they do best – deciding on measures of care. It would remove the hearing from an area where facts are in dispute and which is in any case subject to appeal to the Sheriff. I am sure that hearings would benefit from this clarification of their role. They should certainly not see it as any form of downgrading. The government has reaffirmed on more than one occasion, its confidence in the existing system of juvenile justice and I do so now. This is not, however, to say that it is not possible to introduce measures to improve and streamline our system in order to fit it better for the demands of the future, particularly a future which will see a larger number of contentious child protection cases than in the past.

Lord Clyde recommends that in relation to children who have been removed from home, local authorities should have the same welfare duty as applies under section 20 of the 1968 Act for children who are in their care. However, he thinks that an order should be sought from the Sheriff to make explicit those aspects of control which are only implicit in the existing legislation and are regarded as within the local authority's discretion. It does seem right not only from the point of view of children and parents but also for the reassurance of local authorities, that such matters as access, medical examinations and disclosure of the child's whereabouts should be subject to an order. This would be a very considerable change and would involve spelling out in the law matters which are at present no better than implicit. However, we are sure that there is need for clarification in this area, where the Child Care Law Review has already identified the need for change.

Finally, there is the serious question of situations where the social work department's knowledge and evidence would not justify the drastic step of removing a child from home, but there is sufficient concern to warrant getting access to a child to assess his or her condition. Normally, one would expect that parents would collaborate with social workers, but in the event that such collaboration was not forthcoming, it might be neccessary to have recourse to some form of order to ensure that the child could be examined or assessed in a particular way, in order to deal with genuine concerns about his or her situation. This points to development of something akin to the Assessment Order which has been introduced in England by the Children Act 1989. It does seem a useful fall-back to enable social work departments to have examinations carried out which will, one way or another, deal with the concerns which have arisen about a particular child. Lord Clyde also suggests an order which might ensure the exclusion of a suspected abuser from a household. He suggests that these two orders might be part of a range which he describes as 'Interim Protection Orders', embodying a wide range of powers of an interim nature for the purpose of investigation, or for the immediate protection of a child pending investigation. That is a fairly wide-ranging idea and I would wish to hear the views of different individuals and organisations about the two specific orders and the range of orders before taking proposals for such orders further.

I conclude now by emphasising the need to look forward. From Cleveland to Orkney is a space of four years during which child protection has remained a top priority for all agencies concerned with the welfare of children. It is an area of work which has attracted more than its share of adverse publicity. This could easily lead to an over-defensive and indeed negative reaction from those services which have worked hard to protect children from harm. Lord Clyde has presented his report positively – and we have an opportunity to move forward positively.

For our part in The Scottish Office, we are aiming to produce a White Paper on Child Care Policy and Law early next year and taking action in various ways to prepare for and complement it: we have established working parties on social work practice guidance and on joint investigation and interviewing; we shall be issuing a consultation paper on emergency protection; we are revising interagency guidance and we are investing heavily in in-service training. The new Social Work Services Inspectorate will play an important part in promoting high standards of professional service. All this reflects our agreement with Lord Clyde that child protection is not just a question of getting the legislation right, but providing the right guidance and training.

There is no doubt that working to protect children from abuse is a necessary, complex and risky business. It will continue to present a challenge to all who are concerned with the welfare of children. Lord Clyde makes frequent references to Lord Justice Butler-Sloss's report. We now have an opportunity to build upon the wisdom of both reports, amending legislation and taking complementary action which will help to shape child care for the future.

DISCUSSION

Brian Balcombe
Chair of Social Work Committee, Grampian Region

'Given that in your concluding remarks you stress the importance of the right guidance and training, and that you also praised Lord Clyde's report for the careful consideration shown in that report, would you be prepared to move from the immediate rejection by your government of the recommendation for a three-year qualification course for social workers and perhaps to give this issue more careful consideration, possibly through discussion with CCETSW, ADSW and COSLA?'

LORD FRASER

'Lord Clyde has made observations on that particular recommendation of his that the proposal was not a new one, and with that I agree, and he has said that the response immediately from the Secretary of State was predictable. I suppose I have to agree with that also. What I would want to stress though is that if you were to move to a three-year training programme for social workers, undoubtedly that has significant resource implications, but what I think is important at the present time is to focus upon this area of social work which has attracted the most adverse public response and hostility and if I may say, has rather influenced the general views going beyond child protection and child abuse circumstances to colour public attitudes to social work as a whole. What I would suggest as appropriate is that until such time as resources will permit a move towards a three-year training, we should focus as best we can on our post-qualifying training in relation to child protection. There has been a commitment made on that already, not least with the commitment to training provided at Dundee University, but I think that that is the most that I can offer in addition to the other funding that has been given to the island authority and the extra expenditure for training given to local government.'

David Colvin
Scottish Secretary of BASW

'We are very sorry to hear that remark. I think perhaps some consideration of ways and means out of the impass of simple government rejection of three-year training should be sought and I would suggest that some further discussion is required of that. I would like to ask you an allied question which is recommended by Lord Clyde again, and that is about the establishment of a social work council. Proposals are well advanced for this. We at BASW regard it as essential for the future development of the profession. Would you give it your support?'

LORD FRASER

'Can I respond to the broad issue which I think Lord Clyde also addressed in his remarks to you today, that some investigation might be made, though government considers at the moment that resources are not available to undertake that extension of a full year to basic training where there might be other ways by which it is taken forward. I think that in the first question addressed to me there was a suggestion that there might at least be some further discussion about that. I am certainly prepared to undertake such discussion with anyone wishing to take it forward. What I think would be wrong for me to do would be to indicate, because I cannot do so in the present circumstances, that there would be an undertaking which would be deliverable of a third year. If you are asking if I agree to discussion and participation to improve and extend training beyond the measures which I have already indicated, yes certainly.'

Alison Newman
Scottish Legal Adviser for BAAF

'I would like to ask the present speaker – indeed I would have asked Lord Clyde if I had had the opportunity to do so – what their operational definition of justice is. There is often a distinction made between procedural justice as justice that concentrates on getting the procedures right on paper, and substantive justice which looks at a much wider range of matters including the outcome, whether or not the process gets the answer right, the access to the process of the system, the manner in which the process operates and the timescales. I would be interested to know, as we haven't had a definition of justice I think from either of the speakers, how they would define the concept.'

LORD FRASER

'Others may wish to supplement the answer that I give to this question which, as Lord Clyde suggests, has sought an answer since the time of Plato. If I could just go back to what I said in describing what seemed to me to be an artificial dichotomy that is sometimes expressed in terms of our system: do we have a welfare system or do we have a justice system, and I don't think one should try and drive too hard in either direction. I can say no more that this, there has to be a balance in the way we take things forward. But I was at pains to stress that I would not consider it to be justice if only the outcome appeared to be right. What I was keen to emphasise, and I think this is what we have to examine very carefully as we look to Lord Clyde's proposals for interim protection, in one way or another that at all stages there is a balance sought between welfare and justice. It is potentially enormously damaging if you neglect either party however keen we are to arrive at a broad notion of justice at the end of the day.'

LORD CLYDE

'The procedures in our law and our practice, must always be seen as servants and not as masters. They are the route towards what we conceive and cannot analyse or define as justice, and I think you will find that certainly at the heart of the Scottish system of law there is an element of equity, or justice if you prefer that term, which runs through it, which ought to frustrate any attempt by procedure, if there was any conflict, from having the upper hand.'

Roy Breustedt
Save the Children Fund, Care and Justice Unit

'The point has been made that given the complexity and sensitivity of child sexual abuse, we need more training for social workers and the police. If Sheriffs are to have an increased role, which with respect may require more than a degree of objectivity or an ability to keep solicitors in check, is there a need for further training for Sheriffs, for example, in the ethos and practice of the children's hearings system, as well as the troubled subject of child sexual abuse? If training would be acceptable, where might it come from?'

Lord Fraser

'Can I say once again, I do recognise and appreciate the requirement there is for a very expert degree of understanding of how to interview children, and that came from an earlier question from the police. If there is to be an increased focus on the role of the Sheriff then, yes I think that Sheriffs ought to understand very clearly what are the delicate points in our system. Whether they always exhibit such a delicate understanding is for your own judgement. What I would say though, is that if we are to make a legislative change or indeed for the time being, continue with our existing practice and law, I believe that Sheriffs through their own association would be very anxious to ensure that their understanding of all parts of the system is as good as it ought to be. I am aware that they have in the past undertaken such specialist training, I have heard quite a lot about it. If you have a particular proposal to advance, I am sure the Sheriffs' Association would be very interested to hear.'

Margaret McKay
Childline Scotland

'The minister stated that it is his intention to bring forward a White Paper on Child Care Policy and Law early next year. His commitment to legislation is welcome on the understanding that it is comprehensive, that it will integrate public and private law related to children and that it will be firmly rooted in the principles of the UN Convention on the Rights of the Child. Does the minister agree that the time has now come for a comprehensive Children Act for Scotland covering both public and private law and incorporating the work of the Scottish Law Commission? Will the minister confirm that when such legislation does come forward, sufficient parliamentary time will be made available for such a major piece of legislation and that children in Scotland will not be short-changed because of pressures on the parliamentary timetable?'

LORD FRASER

'I was anxious to stress in my opening remarks that what would be covered in the White Paper and what we intended to cover in legislation in the future would go beyond the area of child protection, however important it may be to secure amendment for example, of section 37 of the 1968 Act. No, our intention is to have a broad Child's Act for Scotland. I think we ought to reflect carefully just how far we want it to go: whether it should seek to be all-embracing in the way that you have suggested. I should say for example, that it has been proposed to me that such a bill as presented to Parliament would be acceptable, but I have to say there are also those who think that to attempt to go into such an area as that really would leave us with a massive blockbuster of a bill not so much a matter of securing sufficient parliamentary time if we are to cover all of those issues, I think I might have some anxiety that the detailed issues would not be as carefully addressed as might have been. Just exactly what the format of the legislation would be remains to be determined but as I concluded in my opening remarks there are some foundations in 1968 on which to build; it is not to knock down that whole edifice and start again.'

Susan Clark
National Foster Care Association

'I would like to thank Lord Clyde for his comments in his report concerning foster care. I would like to address to Lord Fraser, again about the issue of resources – resources for the recruitment, assessment and training of foster carers in the difficult area of looking after children who are alleged to have been abused, particularly sexually abused. What can we hope will come out of this?'

LORD FRASER

'Well, we've heard what Lord Clyde had to say and I don't underestimate how important it is that when foster parents get involved in such matters, they should appreciate clearly what is required of them. Throughout the discussions I have had today, I have indicated I think there is little disagreement between Lord Clyde and myself and what he had to say in his report. I think there is only one matter on which I would like to reflect further in his report. This is the position as regards what might be said by children to foster parents while they are with them. Lord Clyde offered the observation in his report that all agencies (I think I am right in saying) took an exaggerated view of the risk of contamination of evidence. In the particular circumstance of the Orkney Inquiry, I offer no comment on that. I have to say, going back to my previous experience as a Law Officer, I do have my concerns that contamination of evidence is a very real issue. What attracted public attention and disquiet on this occasion was rather a different matter, but it's not difficult to see in the future, some circumstance where a trial came shuddering to a premature end because the evidence that had been secured was, in one way or another, attacked as being contaminated. Just exactly where the balance is to be struck, I think is very difficult. But one particular area from my experience as a Law Officer where it is very tricky is when children have spontaneously said things to a foster parent and what should be done then in deciding whether or not to question further or hold back. But it is just because of such difficulties I recognise of course the point put to me that where foster parents are looking after children who have allegedly been subject to sexual abuse, they should very clearly appreciate the difficult task that comes.'

David Sandison
Solicitor, RSSPCC

'I want to ask you this: if there is greater legal involvement in the process relating to the Child Protection Order, there may well be an early apparent risk of conflict between the parents' interests and the child's interest. How would you see that being resolved? If you have a hearing before a Sheriff where a solicitor is asked to respresent parents, I am not entirely clear that the solicitor will have a duty to look separately at the interests of the child, and I wanted to know what views you could express on the help that could be given to the court, or whether the court could make a request for separate assistance to represent the child if it becomes appropriate that assistance may be needed and that there may be an apparent conflict between the needs of the parents and the needs of the child.'

LORD FRASER

'I would have hoped that if the solicitor acting saw in any way that such a conflict was arising that that would be intimated to the court, and I would also envisage it would not be beyond the court to identify early on, that there was a possibility of such a conflict and indicate that representation might be required.'

DAVID SANDISON

'This relates to the role of the safeguarder. The reason I ask is that I would imagine that maybe it would be more necessary if there is a greater legal involvement because of the tightening of the rules in obtaining these orders. I think you are going to find there would be more lawyers involved obviously, because of the suggestion of the greater use of a Sheriff, and I just wondered what Lord Fraser's views would be on providing the availability of safeguarders or curators.'

3

FROM CLEVELAND TO ORKNEY

Rt. Hon. Lord Justice Butler-Sloss

It is a very great pleasure for me to be invited to take part in today's extremely important conference. I am very conscious of course that I come from a legal discipline and a legal framework which is entirely different from that which takes place in Scotland, so any comments which I make are with some degree of trepidation. I would like first to congratulate if I may respectfully do so, Lord Clyde and his careful, comprehensive and very clear report.

I intend to make a few introductory comments and then take a number of issues which were raised by Lord Clyde in his report, which echo Cleveland and with which I would like to underline my wholehearted agreement, and then be brave enough in a Scottish audience to tell you just a little about the Children Act of which I played only a small part. But we do actually think the Children Act is on the right road and I would quite like to tell you something about it, conscious though I am that this is operative in England and not in Scotland.

The subject on which you have asked me to speak today is 'from Cleveland to Orkney', and the story of nine children removed on a single day, in the early morning, from their homes on the island on suspicion that they were victims of organised sex abuse, is on the face of it far removed from 121 children removed over a period of weeks, most of them removed on the belief of two paediatricians as to the infallibility of physical signs indicating serious anal abuse. What on earth do the two reports and inquiries have in common? But as I read the report however I had a weary realisation that in the approach to and management of the nine children, this might be described as 'Cleveland Revisited'.

The report reveals a depressing and disturbing resemblance, four years on, to many of the criticisms made in the Cleveland Report. It was even more depressing to realise that no-one in authority appeared to have read the earlier report, but no-one even seemed to have read or observed the comments on the

Cleveland Report in serious publications which have been circulated since 1988.

I would like to comment upon some of the problems which Lord Clyde has dealt with and the first of these is the existence of abuse. He reminds us, as we need to be reminded, that it is not widely recognised, outside the audience in this hall, that abuse really exists. I find this so extraordinary, because in the last hundred years or more, there have been in the criminal courts many cases of children who have been raped, children who are victims of incest, children who are victims of anal abuse, children who are assaulted: all of that is obvious, but because it appeared in the criminal courts up till about the sixties and seventies, it was thought to have nothing to do with what is now seen as physical and sexual abuse of children. But it is all the same thing in a different court but with the same children. We do need to recognise that abuse is there and we have to meet the challenge of protecting our children.

I care passionately about the way we treat children when the state intervenes. Somehow or other, inquiry after inquiry, and the Clyde Inquiry is no exception, realised that children need protection, but there seems to be an ignoring of the elementary principles of caring for people. In this case this involved taking children out of their beds, not telling them what was happening to them, leaving them in fear that they might never see their family again, not able to take a change of clothes, their toys. And not allowing them to write to or to receive letters from their parents or even to see their parents for weeks, meant that no consideration was given of each child as a separate individual with special needs and individual feelings. All of this, except perhaps being taken out of their beds at seven o'clock in the morning, we found in Cleveland and some of the children there were kept away for five months or more. The observations have been made again and again by Lord Clyde on the United Nations Convention on the Rights of the Child. We in the United Kingdom are signatories to that Convention; we would then perhaps hope, compared with the Third World, that we do quite a good job for our kids. But we don't do anything like good enough and we ought to be, each of us, very worried about the way in which we fall below standards that our country has signed as being the minimum standards for our children.

The next area I would like to move on to is the instant, sometimes called 'knee-jerk' reaction to an identified problem. I do worry about the issue of a Place of Safety Order which is planned for two and a half weeks. Isn't there any other disposal of children than to remove them as an emergency after two and a half weeks? The sexual abuse alleged was organised sexual abuse but though sexual abuse is serious, does it have to be treated differently from physical abuse? There is not usually the same need to remove children on the instant. There has to be a different response to different types of abuse and of course to different degrees of seriousness. There was in Orkney, as there was in Cleveland, no interdisciplinary approach to the problem, no consideration of widely accepted principles of good practice. There was as in Cleveland, a lack of consideration as to whether the allegations made could be proved and what might be the effect on children of being removed precipitately; of being kept away for weeks or months and then returned home because the allegation that they were abused could not be proved.

If they had not been abused before they went into care, it must surely be a form of administrative abuse to have kept them away in those circumstances for so long. If they have been abused and then sent home because it can't be proven, what are those kids going to think about the system? It is not going to be very easy to protect those children in the future if abuse eventually becomes discovered, and you have already taken them away and failed to prove it. There are three situations of children; there are children who have been abused and you can prove it, and those children sooner or later you will be taking away from home unless you can produce a good system of protection for them in their own home. Then there are children who haven't been abused – you have to be careful that you recognise they have rights. Then there are also the children who may have been abused and you can't prove it. And social workers, doctors, nurses, teachers, health visitors, the police and all other people who care for children and try to protect them have to live like the lawyers, without certainty, with a very real fear, that a child has been abused and needs to be protected, but a solid, calm assessment that you can't prove the allegation and you won't be helping the child in such a case by taking the child away from home and sending him back again. Now it is very hard for people who care to live with uncertainty but we all have to do so.

I read with great interest and some degree of sadness what went on in the Orkneys because with my assessors in the Cleveland Inquiry, I watched 40 hours of interviewing on video and very depressing watching it was. We need to be sure as Lord Clyde points out, what is the purpose of the interview of the child? Is it for investigation? Is it for assessment? Is it for therapy? And as Lord Clyde added, is it intended as a supportive interview? It doesn't matter in a way what you call it, so long as you know why you are doing it. So the police who presumably are investigating and the social worker with the police would probably be likely to do an investigatory interview. Once you get the clinical psychologist and the child psychiatrist in, you must be clear what they are doing and whether it is going to be used for court purposes. If you are going to use it for court and not for purely therapy purposes, you must be sure that certain basic rules are observed such as not suggesting to the child 'Did Daddy put his penis up your vagina?' in suitable language for young children. That, as all of you know perfectly obviously, if the child says yes, it is not going to be very much use in a court of law, but there are variants of that which are used in interviews which are unhelpful. So you would start from the fact: what is the purpose of the interview? You work out the way in which you conduct the interview, so it is open ended. You start without any preconceptions as to whether the child has or has not been abused. I am so relieved and grateful to see that Lord Clyde is talking about the importance of listening to children. Listen very carefully to what they say but don't uncritically accept every word. Apart from anything else, I wonder why it is that some of the most caring people interviewing children believe the child who says that something has happened, but is not prepared to believe the child who says that nothing has happened. Aren't they entitled to the same degree of listening whether it is yes or no? But there are all too many people now in the United Kingdom who only believe that which is said has happened and not that which has not. So please, we have to allow for the denial of these children and accept it.

Coming again to what I was saying earlier about living with uncertainty, if the child denies, it may be for one of two reasons. One is because it didn't happen, the other is the child is not prepared to tell you. It may be that if the child is not prepared to tell you then you don't have any other evidence and you must let that child stay at home; you must keep an eye on the child and hope that one of these days the child will have the time, the space and the opportunity to get help from the grown ups. The arrangements for and structure of interviews is absolutely crucial. If you want to use the interview for any sort of proceedings please video it. Please have a decent form of video. Don't video the bottom of the feet, or tops of the head, or people's backs because what you want to see if you are looking at it, speaking now as a judge trying cases, is the interaction between the child and the questioner. If you don't see the whole of the child or the bit of the child that matters you very often can't hear very much of what the child says because they very often don't want to say anything. You are then denying that video very much use. There is an invaluable book by Dr David Jones of Park Hospital in Oxford called 'Interviewing the Sexually Abused Child' and I do believe it ought to be required reading for everybody who is ever going to interview any child for the purpose of investigation, specifically for the police and for social workers.

I also endorse what Lord Clyde said about what we do with the tapes after they have been recorded, there is a real worry here. I don't know how many of you know that the court welfare officers' reports in the South of England do find their way around pubs and are read out by various people. It is within the realms of possibility that someone may get hold of some of those videos and use them for private viewing. We have really got to treat these tapes with a great deal of care.

Would I be totally out of form to say that parents are human? Parents have rights, we ought to keep looking at the needs of children in the context of the family. Even the dreadful parents (and there are some), we all know are entitled to consideration and until you know if they are dreadful they are entitled to the consideration of anybody who has not been found guilty of whatever allegations have been made. They must be treated with consideration even when the children have to be taken away from them, and they do deserve some support after the event and during the period that the investigations are taking place. The lack of parental support in Cleveland was infinitely worse, though the lack of parental support in the Orkneys was perhaps partly due to the fact you are dealing with so many more parents. But in both inquiries the parents got short shrift and it is not fair, and even if they have been found guilty of every conceivable allegation which has not found any space quite rightly in Lord Clyde's report they are still entitled to consideration.

So, indeed, are the social workers who are under stress where they are dealing with abuse, sexual abuse, physical abuse, emotional abuse, serious neglect of children. It is a very upsetting and stressful experience and the worry as to whether they can adequately protect children who are their first responsiblity is an area which is in my view insufficiently recognised. I understand nothing whatever about social work practice and that part of my report was written largely by a social work director. But I do know that line management is very important. I don't know, as Lord Clyde suggested, how a director of social work gets support, I do know that middle management and those at the coalface need it, and I don't think they get it often enough. I was interested to hear a question from the Foster Parents Association because on my list of people who need support are foster parents, particularly the foster parents of children who are said to be abused. They ought to be getting, it seems to me, both in the Cleveland Inquiry and the present one, more information, more support, more understanding of the particular problems of the children who may be going through even greater trauma than perhaps children normally coming into care.

There are two points in connection with training which I want to make: I unreservedly endorse Lord Clyde's recommendation for a 3-year training course for social workers and the sooner the better. I would also however like to tell you about the training of judges because my view is that judges need training. That view is very much supported in England. We have a Judicial Study Board which introduced for our Children Act an intensive series of courses of training for our judges. This included training by directors of social services, paediatricians, consultant psychiatrists, court welfare officers, guardians *ad litem* and professors of law. One group of people we did not ask to train the judges were our judges, because in this particular field of children, bearing in mind the various reports we had in England, we believed it was very important that we should be exposed to the other disciplines. We believe it is important to have both further training within our own disciplines and a moderate degree of input from the other disciplines engaged in the same work of trying to help children. I would like to see help for children who have been found to be abused, children who have been abused physically, sexually, or administratively. Those children all need some counselling and some help. Some children who have been sexually abused need a great deal of help and the therapeutic work available for children who have been abused around the UK is inadequate, haphazard and patchy. If we don't help our children who have been abused, we will perpetuate the cycle of abused children becoming the abusing parents of the future. We are currently concentrating understandably upon prevention and protection. We must not assume we have done our duty when we have found that a child has been abused. There is a whole lot more that needs to be done in the future. We also need to do something about the abusers and I was very interested to read Lord Clyde's report on the suggestions that within the framework of the law we ought to be able to achieve the situation where the abuser would know, for instance, if he would go or be likely to go to prison or if he was to have the chance to have appropriate therapy. I am very interested in the idea that the Child Assessment Order should include turning out the abuser. This we do on a voluntary basis in England and it is under consideration, I understand at the moment, without any decision.

May I be so bold as to make a comment about the press. There is enormous value to be gained from the press making public unacceptable practices related to children. If we didn't have an independent press who fearlessly go round seeing what is wrong we would be the worse for it. But there should be some discretion, some limits, some curb of our enthusiasm so the story does not have to stay on the front page and sell newspapers at the expense of families and children. The press bear a great responsibility for seeking out what goes wrong and an equally great responsibility for acting moderately in that which they find – which has not been followed either in Cleveland or in the Orkneys. There appears to have been an ignoring of a wider perspective in each of the inquiries of which we have been talking today, a lack of common sense; a lack of ability to communicate; a lack of humanity by good, caring people who devote their lives to looking after other people. Social workers however, in Orkney were, I thought, quite remarkably unlucky. As Lord Clyde pointed out, they attracted the whole of the opprobrium with not a word of criticism of the police from the press.

May I turn very briefly to the Children Act. It was enacted last year as a reforming and comprehensive Act which repeals at least five Acts and most of a considerable number of others. It integrated then under one umbrella the major child legislation with the marked exception of adoption. Listening to Lord Fraser, you would think that in order to get a comprehensive Act you have to include everything. We do include in England both public and private law under the same umbrella. The Act has only been in force for a short period so its implications are so far unclear but what it stands for is neither a charter for families nor for children. It attempts to balance the need to underpin the family unit and to provide some protection to families and protection of children. The welfare of the child is paramount in section 1 and there is an underlying philosophy that parents have parental responsibilities rather than parental rights. Children are seen as people whose parents are responsible for them rather than pieces of property whose parents move them from one place to another. There is a concept, which I hope will work through, on cooperation and partnership between social workers and parents. Nowadays, a child can only be committed to care by a court order. We have new Emergency Protection Orders which include a number of safeguards, which were patently absent in Cleveland and do appear to be absent from the Orkney problems which include that parents could go to court after 72 hours and apply to have the emergency order set aside. There is also the power of the court to order medical and psychiatric examination and assessment. There is the assumption of continuing access or contact between the parent and the children from the moment they are taken away unless the court says otherwise. So five weeks or five months without seeing the parents would be impossible without a court order under the English Act. We haven't yet had time to see how the Child Assessment Order works, but it is a useful alternative to the Emergency Protection Order. Children are entitled to contact with their parents in care unless a judge or magistrate has said otherwise. Delay is detrimental, and there is a careful timetable. I have not known of an Act of Parliament previously that specifies in the first section that delay is detrimental to the welfare of the child. There is an overall duty of the court to have regard, in particular, to the ascertainable wishes and feelings of the child concerned considered in the light of his age and understanding and this applies to care proceedings as much as private family proceedings. Now children have the right to refuse to have medical or psychiatric examination when they are taken into care.

Finally, I would like to say that guidelines are needed which are relatively simple to follow and allow for a degree of flexibility to meet the individuals' problems rather than too great a rigidity. They also need to be dealt with in such a way that those on the ground and at the coalface have told to them what is actually going on. There is no point having, if I may say so, guidelines thrown into the wastepaper basket by the assistant director of social work. What is needed are guidelines which are actually presented to everybody with someone there to tell them what they are about. We have all gained from Lord Clyde coming and telling us about his report. However good guidelines are, people don't read them. What you have got to do is communicate them and there has got to be somebody around (and I know there is no time, and I know there is no money), but guidelines produced through the post without somebody there to explain them is not really going to meet the problem.

I would like in conclusion to underline what Lord Clyde said about social workers. We must remember that social workers are in the front line of supporting families in need and children who require protection. Without them, the community is lost. In making our critical comments and levying criticism at individuals or social work departments there must be some understanding of the difficulties they face in carrying out their onerous duties. Criticism must not be wholly destructive. We must not overlook the work daily carried out by social workers caring for children and helping parents which demonstrates the successful and welcome intervention that they give to so many families. The lapses from good practice should not blind us to the general work of social workers both north and south of the border.

My last comment is this – a plea for communication between groups, between individuals. We live in an age of instant communication but that instant communication which we see in the hall today does not in fact find its way into what is communicated. We might reflect on how inadequate communication is on important topics such as those we are discussing today, and how inadequate that communication is is demonstrated by what goes wrong after people thought, as we thought in Cleveland, that perhaps something like Orkney could not happen. I leave you with this thought: how do we improve our communication skills?

DISCUSSION

David Spicer

Assistant County Secretary, Nottingham County Council

'My question is related to the role of lawyers in the process of investigation. Whatever investigations take place, inevitably, they come under the forensic examination of the courts. Is it not time that there was a very firm recommendation that careful examination, the testing and careful checks that have to be imposed, should take place throughout the process of the investigation? The cost to the Legal Aid purse certainly of picking over the practice which has taken place retrospectively is very damaging, not only to the children who are concerned but it is very delibitating to the professionals to go through that process. I feel that both the Cleveland Report and the Orkney Report really show the need for specialist child care and prosecution lawyers to be involved at the points where they really are going to be of most use to improve the quality of the work: that is, the beginning of the investigation and throughout the process.'

LORD JUSTICE BUTLER-SLOSS

'I'm not qualified to deal with crime I would only say this, that we have a difficult balance in the criminal court between the welfare of the child and the right of the person who is innocent until he is proved guilty or in Scotland, non proven. North and south of the border, people are entitled to a trial and they are entitled to the evidence being proved before a jury. I cannot see how the prosecuting lawyers deal with that at an early stage. But coming to an area with which I am more familiar, in a child care application or indeed even between parents where the allegation is one of sexual, or physical abuse, the court really does have to try the case at that time. It may be that courts can be tougher as to the extent to which they will allow what may be unnecessary cross-examination. I find it difficult to see how the work which is done by the lawyers can be done in the absence of those who will eventually actually make the decision: which is either the jury or the judge. Unless we are going to have investigating magistrates as in the French or other continental system I really don't see that we can do that. One aspect of the Children Act which I hope will be underlined in England at least, is a far greater intervention by a judge or magistrates to directing everyone's attention towards what is necessary rather than raising credit by attempting to destroy cross-examination. But I think we're a long way from moving to what you're saying and I have my doubts.'

DAVID SPICER

'Yes I suppose what I am asking for is an indication that our social work colleagues should have expertise or legal input throughout the investigation so that it does not come under the scrutiny at the end of the process, but they can call on the legal expertise at appropriate points just as they call on psychiatric and other expertise.'

LORD JUSTICE BUTLER-SLOSS

'As I understand it, all local authorities have local authority lawyers and I believe that those local authority lawyers who are members of various legal organisations are taking part. In particular I know solicitors are doing training on how best to meet the challenge of the Children Act. It is not just the judges who need the training, the bar are having training, solicitors are having training so that they will respond also. In local government, lawyers will be available, subject to resource implications no doubt, to help them and they will be called in by social workers.'

Chief Inspector Blue
Northumbria Police

'Does the speaker agree that in England we have fallen short of the recommendations of Pigott in our handling of child witnesses? If so, what lessons can we pass on to our Scottish colleagues to avoid this when drafting legislation?'

LORD JUSTICE BUTLER-SLOSS

'The Scots are getting it, and we're not – that's what's so disgraceful. Pigott is coming into Scotland, as I understand it from a recent response by either the Lord Advocate or the Solicitor General for Scotland who has answered this question in Parliament to say that in Scotland, Pigott is being introduced, but it's not being introduced in England. That's what I understood as the current state of affairs, and since I'm not a politician I will go no further.'

Ann Hollows
National Children's Bureau

'In the Cleveland Report you recommended the establishment of special assessment teams and I note that this is one of the few recommendations which has not been followed through, although I am aware that one area in England has set up a sort of version of this. Do you consider that the availability of this sort of a team would have made a difference to the situation in Orkney or indeed to other cases where there have been particularly complicated and difficult allegations?'

LORD JUSTICE BUTLER-SLOSS

'I'm so sorry but I really don't know the answer. I have this problem that I now sit on the Court of Appeal and I no longer preside over family cases, and I am out of touch with what has gone on in these various matters. I think expert groups going in to advise can obviously from time to time be invaluable and we recommended it. We haven't had it and maybe it would have been a good thing.'

JOHN CHANT

'I think I could help people to recap about the Cleveland proposals for special assessment teams. The suggestion was that the police, social work and the health service should identify those members of their staff who have special skills in the area of assessing child sexual abuse. Those named people in difficult cases or cases that were especially complex should, as it were, be allowed to come together as a professional group to form a professional assessment of the situation. In a sense the idea was to create a bit of space from the statutory responsibilities of those various agencies to allow people to use their professional skills. I think the recommendation as it was put forward was perhaps not well-articulated by ourselves and was certainly neither well-understood nor well-received in that people saw it as an argument for setting up specialist workers to deal with all cases. I leave you to conclude whether or not if that sort of facility had been available, it could have contributed in a constructive way to the difficulties that faced Orkney in coming to a decision about whether or not to intervene.'

Margaret Paterson
Child Protection Advisor,
Blackburn, Hynburn and Ribble Valley Health Authority

'Did the Orkney experience indicate the desirability of a review of the supervisory mechanism available to senior managers in respect of their field staff and their professional practice?'

LORD JUSTICE BUTLER-SLOSS

'Again I speak as an outsider, but I would have thought the answer was yes. But I do say that with a great deal of hesitation because I am not an expert on social work practice on how best one would manage this.'

Michelle Miller
Social worker, Orkney

'Social work has undergone a very thorough and very careful scrutiny by yourselves and there has been a considerable criticism of social work actions following both the Cleveland and the Orkney Inquiries. I was wondering whether yourselves as a legal profession had a comment to make on the actions of the member of your own profession who apparently by his own admission bent the rules. Are you unprepared to comment on the practices of members of the legal profession, yet to comment on other people's professions?'

LORD JUSTICE BUTLER-SLOSS

'You are absolutely right. I commented on the work of social workers as I was invited here to do so but I have been looking at it in the context of the way in which social workers dealt with the problems in Cleveland. If you ask me to comment on some of the decisions in England, I certainly would. I certainly do not know enough about the Scottish system to deal with that.'

Arthur Wood
Chief Executive, RSSPCC

'I would like to ask Lord Justice Butler Sloss and also Lord Clyde if he is willing, if you have any views on the concept of our methods of dealing with controversial child abuse issues when they arise by means of a judicial inquiry. I can only speak from the experience of the RSSPCC but we are a comparatively small organisation in UK terms and the experience of the inquiry put tremendous strains on time, resources and money to the verge of disaster really. I just wonder whether that is a reasonable outcome for an agency which participates in such an inquiry and when one takes into account the total costs and the involvement of legal representation for so many parties, whether there isn't a better and more constructive way of reaching the same kind of scrutiny.'

LORD JUSTICE BUTLER-SLOSS

'Could I possibly ask you what you recommend?'

ARTHUR WOOD

'My own view would be for someone like Lord Clyde, with assessors sitting alone with the authority to bring whoever he pleases before him, to question them, to obtain information about the background to what took place, and to provide a report.'

LORD JUSTICE BUTLER-SLOSS

'If I might speak just for a moment for Lord Clyde who I suspect is in the same position as me, each of us were invited by the government, certainly I was, to conduct an inquiry and I was told what sort of inquiry I was conducting. No one asked me how did I want to conduct this sort of inquiry. I have to say that if they had I would have been astonished because I have never done such a thing before and with any luck I shall not have to do such a thing again. It is an extremely expensive way of dealing with the problem. It does get a problem put on the 'back burner' for those for whom the problem is instantly a worry and it puts on the back burner the judge or barrister or social work official who may be asked to conduct it. There are a variety of inquiries, I should think they are all expensive. The judicial inquiry is particularly expensive because, among other things, it takes myself or Lord Clyde away from what is our ordinary job of trying cases. Once you start such an inquiry, I think it gathers its own momentum and it is extremely difficult to cut down the cost. If you are to have the recommendations which are to have general support, you do have to have people coming to give evidence in the inquiry in the widest possible way, with I think, some assistance to sift the gold from the silt. Where you have, as certainly I had, competing views, I think I had 30 doctors in my inquiry and they did not by any means all agree. I don't know what I would have done with 30 separate views on certain subjects if I hadn't had the assistance of people asking questions on my behalf to see which of the areas really we could get the common ground. In Cleveland we spent our entire time looking between the dissension of the medical profession for the common ground of principles of good practice. Now that common ground has actually been used, as I understand it in guidelines for nurses, social workers, health visitors, and in advice to teachers, a lot of advice to doctors, not only in paediatrics but also police surgeons and general practitioners. There has been a great deal of anxious consultation within the medical profession as to how to cope with these sorts of problems. I don't think that the dozen or more types of disciplines who were pushed into reconsidering their own practices would have done it if we had had a behind-the-scenes private discussion group that didn't carry that degree of credibility. But we were running a very big inquiry dealing with 125 children with this enormous medical dispute. I am not qualified to speak for anything other than a Cleveland type inquiry.'

LORD CLYDE

'If I could respectfully concur with what has been said and presume to add to it. I take all that has been said about the public tradition of an inquiry and its concomitant problems. On the other hand one has to recognise that if you have a private inquiry, it may well lead to public suspicion because something is going on behind doors that nobody knows, and there may be advantages of the public interest if a matter has attracted public attention and public concern to having it ventilated in public even if it is a costly course to adopt. Also if you have a private inquiry, it may well be that one witness may make allegations about another. That other will not be represented, will have perhaps even no knowledge that the allegations are being made and will have no opportunity to defend himself or herself against the allegations and the way in which fairness to that person might be desired. May I just say, that so far as I was concerned, the work I had to do was immensely assisted by the care and labour which the various counsels who were before me spent in assisting me towards the work that I had to do. Without their preparation and their presentation, the whole affair would have taken very much longer and certainly the issues would not have become as clarified as they did. I certainly would not have been able to achieve the publication within the timescale that was achieved without the persistence on the part of the counsel, let alone my assessors.'

LORD JUSTICE BUTLER-SLOSS

'Could I just add something. I do believe the point you are making is a valid one for future consideration. I think governments who invite judges to chair public inquiries which are going to take place in the open should be careful to choose the right case to do it. I think we have got to be very careful that it doesn't come in the popular way of off-loading a very awkward problem which may be by having a public inquiry getting a disproportionate amount of public attention and public money. I don't believe that is true of the two inquiries that are linked here today. I can believe that one ought to be looking in the future very carefully, but it has cost the government a lot of money as well as other organisations, and I suspect that it isn't something that is going to happen very frequently, nor indeed should it.'

ARTHUR WOOD

'Could I just thank you for that response and also in case there is a misunderstanding, make it clear I am not looking for a private inquiry but some creative ideas on a different way of doing it but still in the public.'

4

SIGNIFICANCE OF ORKNEY IN THE UK CONTEXT

(A) ORKNEY AND THE ROLE OF THE REPORTER

ALAN FINLAYSON

In this presentation, I intend to summarise the relevance to today's proceedings of a report which I was commissioned by the Scottish Office to carry out on the ' role and accountability of the Reporter to the Children's Panel' which took eighteen months to complete.

I must make it plain that the piece of work that I was commissioned to do was in no way related to the events which took place in Orkney. The issues about the accountability of the Reporter to the Children's Panel were a subject of interest to the Scottish Office prior to these events. I must, however, say that Orkney has had an effect on the reporter through the heightened public awareness of the Hearing System in general and the role of the reporter in particular in regard to his work, which previously was far from the public gaze. Indeed, when the Scottish Office were considering how to mark the establishment of the 21st year of the Hearing System, they considered ways in which that system could come more into the public gaze. The events in Orkney made such efforts unnecessary.

There are six different topics which I would like to raise briefly this afternoon.

1. The changing pattern of referrals to the reporter and demands on the reporter

When the legislation was enacted in keeping with the principles of the Kilbrandon Report, the public perception was that the Reporter to the Children's Panel would deal principally with cases of young people between eight and sixteen who had committed criminal offences. From the outset, it was recognised that he would have other responsibilities in relation to other kinds of referrals, but in the early days of the system, the vast majority of referrals did relate to offence cases. Over the years, the pattern has changed so that now a substantial number of referrals relate to children who are experiencing a lack of parental care. Such cases involve complex issues, as clearly exemplified by the complexities of the Orkney referrals. It is clear that the time which is taken up with such cases and the responsibilities which the reporters have in regard to the assessment of evidence, their decision-making and their potential appearances in court, are of a very different order to that which obtained in the early years of the system.

2. Heightened public awareness.

The new heightened awareness by the public of the responsibilities which reporters have, which include initiating proceedings which may have the effect of removing children from home, has increased the need for examination of the reporter's accountability. The reporter's role is essentially an independent one because of the quasi-judicial responsibilities which he has. He has got to be somewhat distant from his employers in that regard and he is not accountable, at least for individual decisions, to his local authority. In these circumstances, questions arise as to whom the reporter is or ought to be responsible. If he is not responsible for his decision to his employers, should he be accountable to someone else? The report which I have completed suggests that there is a need to justify public confidence for professional accountability and leads to a proposal that there ought in the future to be an Inspectorate of Reporters.

3. Qualifications and training

In order to justify public confidence and so that reporters discharge their onerous duties satisfactorily, there must be certainty that the right people are appointed to the posts and that they receive the appropriate training to enable them to carry out their duties. So far as training is concerned, reporters for many years have been calling for much more detailed and imaginative training than has been provided in the past. These calls have gone largely unanswered and perforce reporters have required, within hard pressed time schedules, to adopt their own self help brands of training. We have had a suggestion in this conference that self-help training has advantages. So it may, but it also has considerable disadvantages and the report which I have completed repeats the call made by reporters over the years. So far as qualifications are concerned, my report does recommend the establishment of basic minimum qualifications. It does, however, counsel against these qualifications being over-restrictive in regard to requirements of knowledge of law to the possible detriment of understanding child and family development.

4. Support for small authorities

The events in Orkney show that incidents of concern are no respecter of national statistics and that the smallest authority may have the most complex of issues with which to deal. As a matter of accident, in fact, when the events arose in Orkney, they had the benefit of the experience of the largest region in Scotland to assist them in their task. My report does make clear recommendations about the need for small authorities to have clear and accountable systems of support so that complex decisions such as that which arose in Orkney do not fall on one isolated, possibly inadequately trained individual.

5. Variations in reporters' practice

The report by Lord Clyde condescends on certain variations in reporters' practices. My report indicates that these variations can on occasions be quite marked but goes on to stress the value of local decisions being taken to meet local children's needs, while commending an examination of the extent of the variations of practice which obtain and proposing, where possible, an agreed code of practice.

6. Local Authority or central government official

In my report, I outline that the reporter is currently an officer of the local authority. In regard to variations in practice and other issues, including training, there are a number of reporters who believe that the reporter's role ought to become a central government function. Whilst as author I can commend the continued location of the post within the local government structure and comment on advantages perceived to come from such a placement, it further recognises that the future placement of the reporter may be influenced by the forthcoming debate on local government reorganisation.

In conclusion, let me affirm that despite the issues which I have raised, the report, perhaps not surprisingly, concludes that reporters have made a major contribution to the development of an effective system in Scotland for dealing with children who might be in need of compulsory measures of care. As a former reporter, I can make no comment on current practice other than that there is wide variation.

(B) IMPLICATIONS FOR REPORTERS AND PANEL MEMBERS
MARGARET COX

In this brief paper, I will consider the significance of the Orkney Inquiry within the context of the Kilbrandon philosophy and the implications for current reporter/panel member practice. With impeccable timing, a little booklet has recently been published celebrating 21 years of children's hearings in Scotland. It is important to remember that in the late 1960's, Lord Kilbrandon was very much of the view that children were best cared for by their parents. 'If lasting changes were to be made to a child's situation, the participation and involvement of parents in the process were essential.' Indeed, the keywords 20 years ago were 'participation and partnership' – sound familiar?

Before the publication of the Cleveland and Clyde Reports, reporters and panel members had been well aware that the numbers of care and protection referrals had dramatically increased in the past ten years. Reporters, in particular, had sought clarification of lacunae and ambiguities in existing legislation. Significantly, a number of my colleagues have enabled clarification of fundamental issues by stating cases on points of law to the Court of Session.

South of the border, the Children Act 1989 has certainly instituted a legislative shift from parental rights to responsibilities. Given, however, that this ethos was inherent in Kilbrandon's philosophy 20 years ago, it is hoped that proposed legislation for Scotland will clearly define the meaning of the term 'parental responsibility' and provide concepts which are transferable to real life. In addition, we must avoid the creation of 'paper justice' which takes little cognisance of the power imbalances inherent in society. Not only does an abusive parent exercise power over the abused child, but agencies involved in child protection necessarily 'know' how the system works and this knowledge creates inequality in attempting to achieve participative working with families. As is emphasised in the recently published resumé of consumer opinion entitled 'Who's Hearing', we may criticise reporters and panel members, but at least in the children's hearing setting it is often the members who rise to greet the family and not the family who rise to greet the Sheriff!

In determining any child's need for protection, assessment of parental ability is fraught with problems. We must always ask ourselves, 'What does this particular child need to fulfil his emotional and physical potential?' Children suffer when parents are so self-absorbed that they have no emotional space or have difficulty in disentangling themselves from the everyday stresses of life.

The law, however, reflects society's multifarious values and is a social institution based upon power relationships. Any legal process therefore, must 'reduce the complex issues of family life to single choices made on the basis of facts presented.' Whatever reform of the law is enacted, the legal process must recognise that children's rights are not the same as their needs, wishes or best interests. Additionally, rights sometimes cannot fully be protected because of lack of suitable resources or a preoccupation with procedural as opposed to substantive issues. It was after all, the Sheriff who dismissed the application in the Orkney scenario and thereby frustrated the welfare/justice balance of the system already in place.

In considering Lord Clyde's recommendations and the particular implications thereof for reporters/panel members, it must be remembered that his remit was not specifically concerned to explore the basic structure of the Hearings System. In recommending that consideration be given to the review and revisal of the working of children's hearings in the area of child protection, he also stated, 'the problems created by the complexity of sexual abuse cases and the detailed professional consideration of disposal is not met by transferring such cases from the hearing to the Sheriff. The essential element is the expertise of the tribunal be it hearing or Sheriff. The reform prompted by the somewhat special circumstances in Orkney must recognise that in the generality of cases no difficulty or problem has arisen.'

Essentially this comment encapsulates the need to clarify aspects of child care law already addressed by the Child Care Law Review, for example, the role of the children's hearing in determining access in warrants to detain. Lord Clyde, however, arguably frustrates Kilbrandon's separation of adjudication of facts and determination of measures of care by recommending that all children detained via Emergency Protection Orders have their situations examined in the first instance by the Sheriff and not the hearing.

Without elaborating upon the intricacy of the proposed procedural steps of the process and the practical implications for families of greater involvement of the Sheriff, I would emphasise the positive aspects of a hearing's determination of such matters as the law presently stands. If a child is taken into care under place of safety legislation (Section 37 (2)) and the reporter refers this child to a hearing, the further detention of the child does not necessarily rest upon the merits of the evidence in the case. On a regular basis, children are brought to emergency hearings and are allowed home, even when grounds of referral are accepted, because further detention is not thought necessary in the child's interests. We must not fail to distinguish between a social work department being 'justified' in petitioning a Sheriff or JP for authority to remove a child, but there not being a need to detain the child further once his situation has been examined by a reporter or children's hearing. This system of checks and balances does not mean that the initial decision to remove was 'unjustified.' If the law currently lacks an easily accessible right of appeal against the granting of the initial petition to remove a child, the remedy may not be to pass the decision on further detention to the courts where the criterion is based on assessment of evidence and one person's judgement.

Thus although reporters and panel members welcome long awaited clarity in legislation, it would be retrogression to lose Kilbrandon's enlightened approach and the ability of families to participate in decision-making within an informal setting. Will a decision by a Sheriff regarding the continuation of an 'Emergency Protection Order' necessarily involve full discussion with the family? As Lord Clyde has stated, 'In considering the whole question of representation of children and parents before Hearings, sight should not be lost of the need to avoid the introduction of any formal or adversarial character in the process.'

Inasfar as reporters are concerned, there has been historic criticism of our (alleged) lack of accountability. I would suggest, however, that the Hearings System actually incorporates the reporter as integral to the system of checks and balances endemic to current legislation. It is heartening, therefore, to discover that Lord Clyde actually suggests an enhancement of this role in his proposals.

The reporter is an independent assessor and coordinator. As the Cleveland Report emphasises, 'No single agency has pre-eminent responsibility in the assessment of child abuse.' In reality, however, 'no man is an island entire to himself' and reporters cannot function unless other agencies provide accurate information, collected on a methodologically sound basis. Independence of position really only relates to making a final decision about referral or not to a children's hearing and this, of course, must take account of the viewpoint of other agencies involved with any child.

Reporters welcome guidance on 'the exercise of discretion within the framework of accountability'. Practice has developed in accord with the ambiguity of child care law as it stands and some variations in practice have been due to differing interpretation of legislative provisions which in themselves no longer offer a workable structure for the needs and situations of children referred.

In addition, given the necessary emphasis on treating any child as an individual, there must be flexibility which allows for logistical problems of travel in rural areas, differing cultural traditions and values, sufficient opportunity to seek informed legal advice, etc.

In summary, Lord Clyde's report is welcomed as yet another affirmation for reporters of the need to provide definitive legislation which takes account of children's needs and circumstances. For example, when is 'referral' a referral? What is the definition of 'first lawful day'? What are the specific functions of a safeguarder? Please clarify the reporter's role at a hearing!

The paper concept of 'parental responsibility' is fine but what does a panel member or reporter say to a child whose parent recurrently fails to attend a hearing? Referral of a parent for prosecution is rarely in a child's interests. Please define for us, therefore, exactly what is expected but do not lose the benefits gained over the past 20 years. We can always improve on the communication process between child care agencies but must not do so at the expense of Kilbrandon's emphasis on the family's right to participative discussion on the resolution of a child's difficulties within an informal setting.

(C) THE SOCIAL WORK PERSPECTIVE
JOHN CHANT

It is difficult to respond to the issues raised in the report of the 75-day Orkney Inquiry from a social work perspective in ten minutes without running the risk of doing a grave injustice to the people, the issues or the process involved.

Sadly we must acknowledge that there are parallels that can be drawn with Cleveland; it is, I'm afraid, substantially the same lessons, rather than more lessons that have to be learnt.

- The sexual abuse of children by adults or other children is a serious and damaging problem that is difficult to deal with, it is work that requires considerable skill and expertise.
- The interests of children are paramount – their needs are unique and individualised, it is not to their advantage to be treated as objects of concern by well-intentioned professionals.
- To act precipitately on unsubstantiated or unevaluated allegations can be damaging to children, to parents, to social work and social workers.
- The framework of our legal arrangements appear neither to respect the rights of children nor readily deliver justice to parents.
- Inquiries focus on the management and practice of social work and have surprisingly little to say about the shortcomings of the law or its administration.

The fact that lessons from Cleveland were not learnt by staff in Orkney suggests that whilst inquiries may be good diagnostic tools, they are an ineffective way of disseminating knowledge.

Work in this field has significant implications for the training of social workers, their managers and the way their skills are deployed. The government has made its position clear on the question of extending the period of qualifying training.

There is little evidence that the Central Council for Education and Training in Social Work has given the same rigorous scrutiny to child care issues in approving new courses as it has to other matters. The important stance it has taken on anti-racist and anti-discriminatory practice must not be allowed to completely overshadow matters of professional content and practice.

The failure to recognise the increasing complexity of the demands made on social workers is evidenced by the government's resistance to adequately funding qualifying training, and is further compounded by the apparent lack of interest by the controlling authority in the professional content of qualifying courses.

Nor in Scotland has either the central council or The Scottish Office sought to require any form of validation of the training undertaken in this field by local authorities. This is an issue which needs to be addressed.

Notwithstanding the rejection of the inquiry's recommendations about professional training – we need to see further resources invested in training that is properly validated and accredited.

There are many lessons about the exercise of skill and judgement to be drawn from Orkney, not just for social work, but also for the police and for those involved in the administration of justice.

The terms of reference of the Inquiry preclude its consideration of issues beyond the vestibule of the courts. That was a shortcoming of the terms of reference. If social workers do not provide adequate information to support an application for a Place of Safety Order, Sheriffs should not grant them. For a Sheriff to grant such orders on the apparent basis of any one of nine children being the subject of any one of four grounds, and for social workers to be then taken to task, seems like double jeopardy. Social workers appear to be held to blame for the fact that the checks and balances of the law have not worked effectively. There is clearly a training issue for Sheriffs and the judiciary as well as for social workers that needs to be addressed.

Social work in Scotland must acknowledge its misreading if not complacency about events in Cleveland. It is not complacent about the events which took place in Orkney, but it must be emphasised that events in Orkney do not reflect practice across Scotland and it is important that we build on our strengths not our weakness. There is a danger that through inquiries we endlessly refine the standards of social work practice.

The Scottish Office, local authorities, directors and social workers must judge whether the standards implied by the criticisms of the report and its recommendations are attainable within the reality of social work practice in an area office where staff seek to work with a very broad range of client groups. In Orkney, referral to a secondary level service claiming specialist knowledge and expertise does not appear to have achieved the standards implied by the criticism in the report. Are those standards achievable within the present framework of social work practice? How are standards to be validated and practitioners licensed? Is the task we are asking social workers to undertake achievable in the context of the way they are currently trained and deployed? How do we ensure that both practitioners and managers receive the training and support necessary for work in this field?

Some of the leading practitioners in the field from other professional groups have found their experiences in the legal setting bruising. This of itself provides good reason to explore all the alternatives and approach the justice system with caution on this topic. The processes of the law seek to reduce complex issues to simple ones. Are the standards being set by the justice system achievable in the context of the problems which can beset children and their families? The secretive nature of abuse within the family and the need to protect parents from unsubstantiated allegations, require that a threshold is maintained.

Whilst social work seems to have difficulty in learning from the past – the justice systems only seem able to proceed on the basis of precedent. This is a significant issue for practitioners working at the boundaries of existing knowledge. For that reason, social work must take stock.

We now know something of the standards and sophistication that courts will require of our practice and the consequences which can occur when our professional judgement and practice is seen to founder.

We know the consequences of this

· for children – whose real needs can be lost sight of
· for parents – who cannot prove a negative and seek justice; and
· for social workers.

Thorough investigation, careful evaluation and a balanced judgement of the alternatives must always be the precursor to legally based interventions.

Child care practice, including child protection, is as much about working with families as it is about working with children; it is time to reaffirm those basic values and skills in our practice. We are in danger of losing the trust of the people and communities we seek to serve. It is important that we seek to involve, rather than alienate, families.

In absorbing the wisdom of the report's recommendations and the requirements of the justice system, we need to ensure that our practice is first and foremost related to the needs of children and families without losing sight of those situations in which a failure to intervene will leave children at risk of significant harm.

The United Nations Declaration emphasises this commitment in the following terms, 'We will work for respect for the role of the family in providing for children and will support the efforts of parents, other care-givers and communities to nurture and care for children, from the earliest stages of childhood through adolescence. We also recognise the special needs of children who are separated from their families.' Working with parents is the subject of only two recommendations in the Orkney Report.

The inquiry's terms of reference focused it on the action of the social work department and subsequent events, but I was struck by the comments of at least one parent, as reported by a newspaper, to the effect that as well as social work, they felt the law had let them down.

The arrangements of child care law in Scotland are recognised to be in need of review. Rather than some piecemeal amendment and codification we must look forward to seeing the essential element of our provision for children, young people and families reviewed and renewed in Scotland within a Children Act, in the not too distant future.

(D) CHILDREN AS PERSONS

KATHLEEN MARSHALL

The phrase that has echoed down to us since Cleveland is:

'The child is a person and not an object of concern.'

'There is a danger', the report said, 'that in looking to the welfare of the children believed to be the victims of sexual abuse, the children themselves may be overlooked.'

This perceptive statement has often been repeated. But have we really learned the lesson?

If the child is a person, then she is a person with rights.

If the child is an object of concern, he is subject to a consideration which is based on his welfare. But the concern of adults is a mixed cocktail

- of consideration for the welfare of the child
- of concern for the adequacy of the adult's own response
- of concern about fulfilling the requirements of the relevant agency's duties.

Child abuse, and in particular child sexual abuse, touches so many taboos about

- sexuality
- the innocence of children
- the privacy of the family

that those entering the fray are bound to be concerned about society's response to their actions. We are not kind to people who trespass on our taboos. The response that they are breaking one taboo in order to respect another may seem logical but, to many, still feels wrong.

A child who is seen as an object of concern will have decisions about him based on a whole spectrum of considerations, justified by a too facile reference to the child's welfare.

Were the children of Orkney treated as 'persons' or 'objects of concern'? Initially, it appears, they were objects of concern:

- They were removed from home with very little explanation.
- Dissuaded from any substantial dialogue with those who removed them.
- Deprived of personal possessions.

- Forbidden communication with family or friends.
- Kept in the dark about allegations.
- Not permitted to attend children's hearings which were making decisions about them.

There were justifications proffered for these measures:

- the need to remove the children to a safe place where they would feel free to talk
- the need to avoid pressure being put on the children not to tell
- the need to avoid contamination of the evidence.

If you are starting off from the presumptions that:

- all actions must serve the best interests of the child;
- those interests are best served by removal of the child;
- and thus preservation of the evidence,

one can see how the actions can be justified.

But that is a simplistic approach. The problem in dealing with these cases is that the child is the evidence. Protection of the evidence can often mean isolation of the child from all that is familiar.

The problem with a purely welfarist approach is that it is too open. It is too easy for well-meaning people to hold out decisions as based on the welfare of the child, without acknowledging the complicated cocktail of concerns which have imbued the process.

So, the initial actings of the agencies in Orkney were based on concerns about the protection of the children and the evidence.

When the case came before Sheriff Kelbie, there was a dramatic shift in emphasis – away from the children as objects of concern and towards the children as 'persons possessed of rights' as he put it in his judgement. The Sheriff criticised the lack of involvement of the children in the decision-making process, dismissed the case as fatally flawed, and added that, in his view, the children ought to be returned to their parents.

There were statements within the Sheriff's judgement of which a children's rights advocate can only approve. Yet one is left with an uneasy feeling that what happened was not right.

Children are persons – yes. They have rights – yes. But they have some special rights arising out of what the Universal Declaration of Human Rights referred to as their need for special care and assistance. One of these is the right to be protected. I can only reiterate here what the Scottish Child Law Centre said in its submission to the Orkney Inquiry, and that is that

> 'If there is evidence that a child requires care and protection, that evidence *must* be heard. There should be no question of 'getting off on a technicality'. What is at stake is not, as in criminal law, the liberty of an alleged wrong-doer, but the safety and integrity of a child.'

So – a child is a person with special rights, one of which is the right to protection. I have attempted to show how an over-emphasis of protection can degenerate into treating the child as an object of concern. To avoid this, it is necessary to see protection, welfare and best-interest arguments, not as adhering to a welfare model which is in opposition to a rights model, but as forming the content of one particular right which has to be put in the balance along with the other rights of the child – to due process of law when liberty is restricted, to participation in decisions concerning them, to contact with family and friends, to respect for the humanity of the child.

This integration of the welfare and justice models can be achieved by taking, as the basis of any reform of child law, the United Nations Convention on the Rights of the Child, which was ratified by the UK on 16 December 1991.

The Convention sets out four broad categories of children's rights to:
- survival
- development
- protection
- participation in decisions which affect them.

The Convention asserts that children have the right to have their views taken into account in all matters affecting them, and to due process of law when their liberty is restricted – as indeed it is when children are detained in a place of safety, even if it is alleged to be for their own good.

The Convention also says that children have a right to be protected, and that in *all* decisions affecting children, the best interests of the child must be a primary consideration.

The UN Convention took ten years to prepare and is a carefully balanced, child-centred charter, which recognises also the responsibilities of parents and the wider family to give direction, guidance and support to children in accordance with their evolving capacity.

Ratification of the Convention means that it is now a statement of government policy. The government is committed in theory to taking steps to implement it. This commitment is given an added and urgent impetus by the first of Lord Clyde's 194 recommendations which says that:

> 'Reform in the field of child law and in particular in matters of child protection should proceed under reference to the European Convention on Human Rights and the UN Convention on the Rights of the Child.'

So, treating a child as a person means recognition of the rights of the child – both those which the child shares with the rest of humanity, and those which adhere specifically to the child as a person requiring special care and assistance.

Treating the child as a person also means treating the child as a *whole* person, and not as the by-product of adult concerns, and an adult-centred legislative framework.

You have already heard of the many current movements for reform of child law in Scotland. Many worthy bodies have been considering what to do about children, and have sometimes themselves expressed concerns about the limitations of their remits.

The Scottish Child Care Law Review Group referred to several matters not directly related to their remit, but which 'nevertheless had a bearing on it'. (27.2) For example, in relation to health and education, the Review made a number of recommendations about which it commented:

10.2 'These changes will have necessarily limited impact on difficulties which are both major and long-standing' because 'the boundaries of our remit do not allow us to recommend specific duties which bind each of the service agencies.'

1.13 The group recognised the complexity of child care law, and its 'interaction with other legislation – notably that applying to criminal justice, adoption and custody proceedings under civil law, particularly divorce'.

19.3 It pointed out that 'Multiple child care legislation can cause serious problems when there is no established legal provision for relating different child care proceedings',

1.6 and referred with approval to the possibility of a consolidation of the law being undertaken by the Scottish Law Commission.

The Scottish Law Commission has indeed recently produced a report on family law, making substantial proposals for change in the private law and setting out the skeleton of a proposed Child and Family Law Code.

19.3 'There is no reason', the report concluded, 'why Scotland should not eventually have a comprehensive code of child and family law. How this might best be achieved will depend largely on the legislative opportunities available.'

Given the limitations on availability of parliamentary time, the Commission has proposed a modular approach to enacting the various components of the code, culminating in a consolidation which would, it says, 'present the opportunity to introduce some coherence of language and style and to eliminate many spent, transitional, and overlapping provisions.'

Whilst appreciating the pragmatism of the Commission's approach, I believe the time has come to take a stronger stance on the need for properly integrated legislation, centring on the needs and rights of Scottish children. The remit should not be a particular area of the law. The remit should be the child.

The argument of the first part of my contribution was that a framework was needed which would facilitate a careful balance of the rights of children based on the UN Convention on the Rights of the Child. Children subject to multiple legislation are also subject to multiple legal concepts, multiple terminologies, and multiple court orders. We will never achieve a satisfactory balance if what we are weighing includes the apples of private law, and the oranges of public law.

Similar movements for reform in England and Wales led to the drafting of an integrated Children Act. Scottish children deserve at least the same consideration and allocation of parliamentary time. My conclusion therefore is that we have not learned the lessons of Cleveland. Both the actings of agencies and the priorities of government are based on adult concerns, of which children are indeed the object, but sometimes not even the primary object.

We can go some way to remedying this by taking seriously
Lord Clyde's first recommendation and forwarding to the
Scottish Law Commission the conclusions of the current inquiries
and reviews, with a request that they prepare a draft Bill
integrating the substance of public and private law, and centring
such integration on the Articles of the UN Convention on the
Rights of the Child.

(E) THE ROLE OF THE SAFEGUARDER

Stewart Asquith

My comments are much more specific than those of my
colleagues and directly relate to the endhanced role of the
safeguarder as envisaged in the report. They will though have,
I hope, wider implications for child care.

What I have to say should also be seen as an attempt to further
current debate and discussion on the rights of children, their
views and their wishes. The question underlying my comments
– to what extent can the rights of children be best protected
within a system concerned primarily with their best interests –
is of course not new. The further question that is prompted by
the Clyde proposal is whether and in what way an enhanced role
for the safeguarder could have and would have made a difference
to the experience of children in the particular circumstances of
what has come to be known as the 'Orkney Affair'.

Three recommendations from the report can be juxtaposed.
These are:

> **Recommendation 1**—that future developments in child
> law and especially in child protection should proceed
> under reference to the UN Convention on the Rights
> of the Child.
> **Recommendation 82**—that in every case when a child is
> removed under a Child Protection Order, the
> appointment of a safeguarder must be considered.
> and
> **Recommendation 84**—that a pilot scheme should be run in
> order to try out the enhanced role of a safeguarder
> before possible development of a child advocate.

What these recommendations are premised upon is the
recognition of the need to identify an individual with the
responsibility of protecting children's best interests (17.12)
Further, not only are children's interest to be protected (Article

85

3 of the UN Convention) but there is also a commitment to give consideration to the views and wishes of the child in all matters affecting him or her (Article 12 of the Convention) (17.7). The further recommendation that that role would be best carried out by a safeguarder with a wider remit than at present is qualified by the possibility of considering the development of a child advocate.

Now there is an inherent tension in being concerned with both the interests and the views of a child and this is a tension that is perhaps not resolved in either widening the role of the safeguarder nor in the development of a child advocate as discussed in the report.

My own comments draw heavily on the Scottish Child Law Centre presentations to the committee but also on significant contributions to the Justice for Children Conference held in Glasgow in 1992. In particular, Duquette argued on these points precisely in rejecting the safeguarder as being the appropriate person in whom to invest what really are the responsibilities of a child advocate. The Clyde Report is surely right to point to the need for some independent individual to look after the interests of the child. But there are a number of problems in seeking to widen the role of the safeguarder.

Put briefly, the main concerns are whether the enhanced safeguarder role as envisaged in the report can be achieved without qualitatively changing the very function and philosophy of the safeguarder as constituted at present; to what extent the safeguarder or indeed the child advocate can both promote the interests of children and represent their views and wishes; that the Clyde Report does not go far enough and that in the long run, the enhanced safeguarder role would not meet the objectives of the report itself.

In terms of the Act, safeguarders are to be appointed where there is or may be a conflict between the interests of the child and those of the parents, and he or she is to make such inquiries as considered appropriate. The enhanced safeguarder role would include:

- making investigations
- following up cases
- keeping the child informed
- representing the child
- being present when the child is interviewed.

Moreover, in recognition of the new role, more safeguarders should be appointed, there should be more training, and skills required of safeguarders should include law and social work. Safeguarders are not to be appointed in every Child Protection Order, but should at least be considered in every case.

We have very little information on the work of safeguarders at present, how they execute their duties, what kind of cases are they employed in and for what reasons. Curran's research(1989) on the early days of safeguarders is useful here and a number of issues can be identified which must surely form the basis of discussion before a decision can be made about how best to proceed.

1. Safeguarders are not extensively used. Curran, though his work is now dated, points to the fact that in the initial stages of the development of the safeguarder role, it was anticipated that 1000 would be appointed to cases in the first year. Only 142 were so appointed. The general question raised by Curran was whether extensive use could and would be made of safeguarders in the absence of a commitment to their value by the key decision-makers – panel chairmen and Sheriffs. That issue is still to be addressed.

2. Safeguarders are deployed very differently throughout the regions. We lack information on the reasons for such differences, for example, what cases are they appointed to and for what reasons; whether there are any differences in their appointment by Sheriffs and panel chairmen.

3. In the absence of a clear statement of function, there are misconceptions about the role of safeguarders. And this may in part contribute to the low numbers appointed.

4. Relationships between the child and the safeguarder is restricted to particular proceedings and even then does not necessarily involve the safeguarder in the whole process.

5. Lack of clarity of the new role as envisaged in the report and in particular how the safeguarder will resolve the tension between promoting the child's best interests and at the same time representing his/her views and wishes.

6. Enhanced safeguarders are not to be appointed in every case in which a Child Protection Order is made. A number of issues surface here. One is the obvious question of why there should be such a selective appointment of the 'enhanced safeguarder'. If the concern is to further the UN Convention on the Rights of the Child and to marry a concern with interests to a concern with views and wishes, then a strong argument can be made that there should be universality of appointment. Moreover, this should not be restricted only to Child Protection cases but should be extended to other grounds of referral. This is particularly so in a system where there are so very few appeals made to the Sheriff against decisions of the children's hearings.

7. There appears to be a bias in favour of appointed safeguarders having legal qualifications. If this is the case then this begs a number of questions about the function and philosophy of the safeguarder, the skills required and the very nature of the training such individuals should be offered. Nor is it the case that the child advocate should necessarily be legally qualified – as I read in paragraph 17.17. There are a number of internationally available models for non legally qualified child advocates as, for example, the CASA (Court Appointed Special Advocates) as discussed by Professor Don Duquette, and the Children's Hearings System could in fact accomodate forms of these.

In conclusion, Lord Clyde's report in its discussion of the role for the 'enhanced safeguarder' to protect the interests of children does clearly identify the ways in which children's rights and children's wishes can be diminished in formal institutions. And though the enhanced role for the safeguarder is premised upon this concern, there must surely be greater clarification of the role to be played, who best can play that role and what kind of training is required – all this before a pilot scheme can meaningfully be set up.

It would be possible to introduce a child advocate into the Scottish Children's Hearing System with a remit to protect children's interests *and* to promote their views and wishes; who needn't be legally qualified and whose brief would not threaten the philosophy of the children's hearings. But before such a policy is formulated or even debated, much more information is needed about how our colleagues in other jurisdictions have sought to resolve this issue.

We would also do well, bearing in mind the injunction of Article 12 of the UN Convention, to seek the views of children themselves who have had the benefit of assistance from a safeguarder on the nature of that assistance and its value. We have no information at all on the way the role of the safeguarder is either experienced or viewed by children or their families.

One last point. We are encouraged to distinguish between 'taking seriously' what children have to say from believing it. I would want to add that to take them seriously, as adults we have to learn how to let them speak and how to hear them – listening isn't enough. That requires not just the introduction of new initiatives for protection or rights enhancement but rather a significant shift in how we view adult-child relationships and what we expect of our children.

PANEL DISCUSSION
Mary Dundon
Child Protection Manager, Lincolnshire

'As more people come forward to share their experiences of being abused, and as examples of new and more extreme horrors of this subject are revealed, how can social workers move from the position of frantically trying to keep up with the position of being one step ahead so that they are able to provide an informed, pro-active, sensitive response? Perhaps it would be more helpful for inquiries to focus on the nature, cause and expense of a particular aspect, or indeed all forms of abuse, rather than the apparent inability of a particular profession to respond appropriately. This would do more than anything to enlighten and inform both public opinion and the professional response.'

JOHN CHANT

'One of the most striking things for me in the Cleveland Inquiry was the number of letters that have been sent to Dr Marietta Higgs along the lines of : Stand firm. Be brave. Don't let them put you down; this is what happened to me when I was a child. Letters written by people with good education from obviously 'respectable' backgrounds. I think in that context, it brought one face to face with reality of the abuse which many people have suffered within the family and that I think is increasingly the everyday experience of social workers – whether they're engaged in child protection work or whether they are working with people with mental health problems, there is no escape from the reality of that situation. I think the issue about whether or not the way in which we work with those problems would be further developed by the process of inquiry seems to me to be an application of our own professional skill and ownership of our work in this area. What social work needs to do is to look at the way in which we develop our knowledge and our practice base and the way we share that with one another in a way which is validated, and lend its authority to the practice that we undertake because what we have heard all day is that if we don't do that, if we can't be credible in our own practice and demonstrate the authority to the work that we do, inevitably, the rest of the community must question our practice in ways which leave us feeling very misunderstood and defensive. I don't think that is helpful to the client.'

Andrew Girvan
Assistant District Officer, Strathclyde Regional Council

'I would express some concern that the emphasis in the Orkney Report seems to be towards the standards and ways and means of gathering evidence, for example, videos and so on, that lean far more heavily towards the criminal justice system than the children's hearing system, which I think is the one that to date has proven to be the better at meeting the best interests of the child. So there is possibly danger that the notion of the balance of probability seems to be in danger of being lost and I would welcome the views of the panel on that.'

KATHLEEN MARSHALL

'There was a recommendation in the report about making sure that the interests of the child take precedence over the public interest in securing prosecution. I think there certainly is a tension, given that the child is the evidence, that you may reach the stage where you wish to do something that may be for the child's own good but it may make the evidence not very valuable in the prosecution. I have come across cases like that. There was one case where a child was already protected by a supervision requirement and the child was still not being allowed access, even supervised access, to parents on the grounds that the parent, who was suspected of colluding in the abuse, might manage to dissuade the child from saying anything. In our own response to the submission to the Orkney Inquiry, we had said that the interest of the individual child should always take precedence over the public interest. I realise that there are actually difficult aspects to that because there is an argument that the interests of other children in the community are involved as well. You manage to secure a prosecution and then you can do more to protect other children in the community from this particular perpetrator. I think that is a very difficult argument. I think I would still on balance, come down in favour of the interests of the individual child and judge on that basis, saying that for this particular child, what are the benefits or traumas that are going to take place if we go forward with the prosecution. We would have to make a decision on it based on those considerations.'

STEWART ASQUITH

' It seems to me that if you are suggesting that underlying your question is a much broader concern that going down the legal road, the criminal justice road, radically threatens the philosophy of the children's hearing system, then I would share some of that concern. The further involvement of the law, criminal justice and judicial system may well be a threat to the philosophy of the Children's Hearings System.'

Ronald Mair
Geilsland Residential School

'Having shared the five weeks of Orkney with one of the young people involved, I felt concerned at the time that the whole process seemed anything but child-centred. My question therefore is, how do we ensure that the normal principles of good child care practice don't get subordinated to the overriding concern for investigation and protection? I would welcome the panel's views.'

JOHN CHANT

'I think the thing that has disturbed me about these situations when they occur is that if you talk with the staff who are involved, they will almost certainly tell you that the reason for the actions they took were based on good child care. One of the things that is perhaps quite striking, I suspect, in a curious sort of way, both in Cleveland and in Orkney, is that the main grade social workers ended up feeling as powerless as the parents felt about the processes that they were involved in. That I think has some very important messages to give managers in social work departments. How do we take time to ensure that we don't react to ten years of inquiries that were criticising departments for not intervening, by intervening too precipitately. I think the only way in which we can be sure that our practice stays child-centred is to take a small step at a time and to carefully evaluate what we are doing and why we are doing it. I think that is true in a very conscious way because the evidence is that if we don't, we will do things for the best possible reasons, but lose sight of the interests of the individual child in the middle of all of that.'

Jean Raeburn
Panel Training Organiser

'If in the future, as Lord Clyde suggests, the Sheriff is to take responsibility for Place of Safety and Interim Orders, and in so doing is taking decisions about access and about placement, can we really say that this is the same separation of adjudication from disposal with which we're accustomed in the Hearing System?'

MARGARET COX

'I think this was the point I was trying to make in my own presentation, but obviously Kilbrandon very much emphasised the separation of adjudication of facts from the determination of measures to be applied, and my concern would be that the question of the interests of the child would be totally dependent on the assessment of the merits of the case and facts surrounding the initial detention of the child.'

KATHLEEN MARSHALL

'I think this is a very interesting proposal and there is quite a division of opinion going up about it. Certainly when I read it, being a lawyer too, it sounded very logical to me and I think it sounds reasonable that these positions should go to the Sheriff and take the adversarial element out of the Children's Hearing System. But I am very much aware, from talking to people who are operating the Children's Hearing System, that there is quite a strong reaction against it and all I can say about that is that we'll just have to wait until we can get the consultation paper on child protection. I hope we can all keep open minds on it and try and get through all these issues because I think we have to talk about that.'

MARGARET COX

'For sometime panel members and reporters have bemoaned the fact that the ability to look at on-going contact is not part of the current legislation. It is an issue that has been around for sometime and I question strongly whether panel members making time to discuss with the child and the parent, where in fact the hearing doesn't even have the power to put the parents out of the room to discuss matters with the child – whether one can actually say that the hearing makes the process adversarial. I think we have to consider the effects on families of putting such an important point of ongoing aspects, of ongoing rehabilitation of the child, because as someone was mentioning earlier, what happens in the future isn't just about the determination of the initial abuse, it's about rehabilitation for the child the minute the child is taken into care, and we have to look as the best structure for that. I suggest that that structure is the children's hearings."

Paul Brown
Solicitor, Legal Services Agency

'I wonder if members of the panel would like to comment on what the lessons for the legal profession are that come out of this, because this doesn't seem to me to be just a training issue for judges and for solicitors or advocates. More importantly, it relates to what form of legislative reforms should come out of this. It seems to me that the day has pointed to a lot of lessons for a lot of people but none whatsoever for lawyers in the general sense, apart that is from the plain fact that access to justice is undoubtedly severely restricted and we appear to have views that maybe having public inquiries shouldn't happen because of the excessive fees charged by counsel. I think there is a range of issues which deserve debate by all and I wonder why that has not happened. There are two questions: first of all, what are the changes that are needed and secondly, why has no-one discussed them?'

ALAN FINLAYSON

'I thought we had talked about issues today relating to the appropriate forum for these kind of areas. I think we have also touched on the area of training for the judiciary. I think people could also talk about the focus of training for the legal profession and in particular those who are appearing. For instance, it is my understanding that in England, practitioners would require from the Law Society some sort of approbation of their fitness to involve themselves in this task. Many of us would worry about the whole idea of the legal process taking over in the court situation, following along the lines of what it appears, at the moment, that it is extraordinarily difficult for an accused person to plead guilty nowadays. We'll give it a run and see what happens, and if that kind of framework was to come into the child care situation, I think it would be a very, very dangerous one because it could lead to this adversarial thing.'

MARGARET COX

'As a practising reporter of some years standing, I have been enthralled by the fact that the Orkney Inquiry has all of a sudden made a great difference in the expertise and experience of solicitors appearing with the families in the courts. I have been used to, prior to Orkney, in a court setting, often finding a solicitor, representing a parent coming in at the last minute saying, "Can you tell me what this is about?" What I say to members of the legal profession is that perhaps the answer is that some introspection and consideration is required of issues that have been raised today. Certainly, parents' rights don't just deserve the mere presence of the solicitor. Parents' rights demand just as much attention as in any other case.'

JOHN CHANT

'I can't tell from reading the Orkney Report whether the Director of Social Work sought advice from the authority's legal advisor. I can tell you that in Cleveland, the authority's legal advisors in the solicitors' department took part in quite a number of case conferences but they didn't appear as witnesses at the Inquiry – I can't think why, but they didn't. I think, if you like, there is a criticism of the law generally and solicitors in particular, that as a profession working in this field that does not enjoy a status that will bring able people into it on a long-term basis. There is a serious agenda for the law if we are going to have a legal system that is more child-friendly – we won't get it until those who are engaged are able to develop more expertise in this field, and that simply underlines the point we're all making that there needs to be training for solicitors in this area as well as for social workers.'

KATHLEEN MARSHALL

'I think we are in a catch 22 situation here with solicitors' knowledge of child law. On the one hand the system says, we don't want lawyers involved because they make everything adversarial and we do have a welfare-based Children's Hearing System that doesn't particularly encourage solicitors to go to hearings. It doesn't pay them for a start, which is particularly discouraging when you're a normal solicitor. So if you are saying we can't expect normal lawyers, who have to earn a living, to put in a lot of effort learning about child law, if it is not something that they are going to be doing on a reasonably regular basis, therefore we have to say, how much do we need legal advice and legal involvement in these matters? I think some of the experiences of the Orkney inquiry shows that we certainly do need a greater level of legal expertise. But we either have on-going training for lawyers that they get paid to go to and that they may not get very much chance to put into practice, or you actually make a place in the system and you have an expectation where people caught up in the system will get legal advice.'

Orkney Parent

'Just as you have made a remark about paper justice, I am concerned about the paper calls for consultation. We attempted to get a copy of Alan Finlayson's report. In section 10.6 he suggests that the consultation process should be such as to encourage interested individual members of the public who may have observations on any of these issues to contribute their views. We tried repeatedly. I first tried as a parent from Orkney at The Scottish Office to get a copy of Alan Finlayson's report. I was told that it wasn't for the public and so I tried thinking that it was perhaps because I was a parent from Orkney, I tried friends right round the country and nobody could get a copy of the report if they were a member of the public and not a member of the care agencies. Recommendation 38 says that the Secretary of State should encourage the fullest possible consultation process to follow on the publication of this report. Does the panel feel that this recommendation has been properly implemented?'

Alan Finlayson

'Well, I suppose the answer to that must be, "No." I myself am not party as yet, to the results of the consultative process, which I gather finished sometime in the middle of October. But I do know all requests were not being satisfied.'

CONCLUDING REMARKS

Stewart Asquith

In the course of the conference, as can be seen through the contributions and the discussions which followed, three very broad themes can be identified. These are the concern with (a) the rights of children; (b) the whole issue of the adequacy and appropriateness of the training afforded to key personnel charged with responsibility for children; and (c) the removal of children from home.

Both the Cleveland and Orkney Reports highlighted in their own way the need to safeguard the rights of children. The Cleveland Inquiry had stated the principle of viewing children as persons and not simply as objects of concern. What is obvious from the handling of the cases in Orkney, as Lord Clyde himself had commented on, is that amidst the activities which had been prompted by the wish to protect the children, the children had somehow been lost in the proceedings; there was no one charged with the responsibility for ensuring that they were not, ironically, left out of it all. In that respect, the suggestion that safeguarders be given an enhanced role has to be seen in the context of more general debates about how best children's rights might be protected in a system in which their welfare is a primary consideration.

It also touches directly on the more fundamental question, never really tackled in either the Orkney or Cleveland Reports, of just who might be the best persons to carry out such responsibilities, what training might be required for them and whether they should be legally qualified or not. These are general concerns being considered in many countries at present but there is a particular edge to the debates in Scotland because of the philosophy of welfare underpinning the Children's Hearings System. The determination of the skills and expertise required of someone appointed to protect children's rights also has a direct bearing on just how far the law can become involved in the Children's Hearings System without fundamentally threatening the integrity of the Kilbrandon philosophy. Whatever future what might be called the 'enhanced safeguarder' may have, the debates about protecting and promoting children's rights under the aegis of the UN Convention on the Rights of the Child have really only just begun in Scotland. The balance between protecting children's interests on the one hand and allowing them to express their views on the other; taking seriously what children have to say without necessarily believing them, as both the Cleveland and Orkney Reports urge, require the drawing of very fine lines.

Training is an area of major concern and has been so for some time. What is clear from the conference is that training was not seen to be a concern only for social work. Certainly, there was considerable comment and discussion on the adequacy of the skills gained by social workers through their training to allow them to fulfil their professional role in interviewing and working with children generally, but more specifically with those about whom allegations of sexual abuse had been made.

But the relevance and adequacy of the training afforded to other bodies involved, especially the police and the judiciary, was also identified as being an area demanding further consideration. The police and social work welcomed the suggestions about joint initiatives in training and there was also a clear consensus that members of the judiciary should be themselves better qualified for dealing with such complexities as presented in child sexual abuse cases.

However, there must inevitably be a sense of *déjà vu* with regard to training in that many of the statements and proposals made by Lord Clyde in his report echo forcibly those made in the Cleveland Report. Lord Justice Butler- Sloss, in expressing disappointment at the way in which the lessons from Cleveland had not been taken on board, must surely have been speaking for many others. The recognition by the government of the importance of Lord Clyde's recommendation for increased training for social workers, accompanied with the political inability to find the funds necessary, has a history in many reports which preceded even the Cleveland Inquiry.

Social workers and other authorities, in deciding when to apply for removal of a child from home in cases of alleged child sexual abuse, walk a very thin line between being accused of acting precipitately and not acting speedily enough to prevent some harm being inflicted on a child. This is a decision that is dependent upon not just the adequacy of the training undergone by professionals but also upon the knowledge available at particular points in time. It is also a decision which stands at a point of potential conflict between welfare concerns and those of a more judicial or legal nature where the child's interests at that point in time may conflict with evidential considerations.

But when the decision to remove a child has been made, the question arises as to whom, and under what conditions, parents and children themselves may apply to appeal against the decision. The problem presented by Lord Clyde is in his suggestion that the most appropriate person should be the Sheriff, the implication being that this would reduce the role in the whole process played by the children's hearings. Whether the panel members will see this, as Lord Fraser counsels against, as a downgrading of the Hearing System remains to be seen. But what Lord Clyde has reminded us of is the very intricate network of relationships that exists between the Children's Hearings System in Scotland and the courts. In some respects, the ideological tensions between a welfare philosophy for dealing with children and a more judicially or legally oriented approach is being played out in the aftermath of the Orkney Affair.

As Lord Fraser also pointed out, since the Cleveland Report, child care has been a top priority and the process of change and development in practices, policies and procedures is ongoing. The government had expressed its readiness* to accept the majority of the Clyde recommendations and at the time of the conference, The Scottish Office had already established working parties relating to social work and joint investigation and training, and had begun to invest in in-service training. This has to be seen as part of the exercise leading to the publication of the White Paper on Child Care Policy and Law, intended to provide a comprehensive statement leading to legislation and change in child care comparable to the integrated philosophy which underpins the 1989 Children Act.

The process of preparation for the White Paper also included the publication of a consultative document on Emergency Protection of Children in Scotland (February 1993), proposing

*See Hansard 27.10.92.

change in the arrangements for protecting children from harm in emergency situations. Based on the recommendations of the Child Care Law Review and the Clyde Report, the consultative paper also recognised a number of key principles, reminiscent of those which informed the Children Act in England and Wales (See page 2 of the consultative paper). These include the child's right to protection from harm; the parents' basic responsibilities for the child and the rights necessary to exercise those responsibilities; the need for proper justification and legal authority for the child's removal; and the opportunity for the child and the parents to make a full and immediate challenge to removal and detention of the child, with the necessary legal representation.

Reflecting these principles, the consultative paper proposed new orders to replace the Place of Safety Orders, new arrangements and time scales for the operation of such orders, and speedier possibility of challenge by parents and children. Views were also sought on the possibility of having the alleged abuser removed from the home and contact with the child.

The two new orders relating to the removal of children proposed in the consultative paper are the Child Protection Order and the Child Assessment Order. Whereas the Child Assessment Order is to be very similar to the English and Welsh Order, the Child Protection Order is seen to differ significantly from the English Emergency Order.* Following Lord Clyde's recommendations, the consultative paper proposed restricting the use made of Place of Safety Orders under section 37(2) of the 1968 Social Work (Scotland) Act by allowing removal of a child only where there is reasonable cause to believe that a child is likely to suffer *imminent* harm and where immediate removal and detention is necessary for the child's protection (para. 2.4). The English Emergency Order employs the criterion of 'significant' harm.

In recognition of the principle of protecting the rights of the child and the parent, when an order is made, the Sheriff is to have discretion to appoint a safeguarder or curator to the child (para. 2.5) and parents and child are to be entitled to apply for a variation or recall of the order to the Sheriff at any time

*See Emergency Protection of Children SCLC March 1993.

within seven days after removal of the child (para. 2.10). Legal representation would be available for such proceedings.

Again, looking at such proposals from a wider point of view, the consultative paper contained proposals which derive from recommendations and thinking underpinning not just the Clyde Report, but also the deliberations of much earlier inquiries, as well as key principles offered by such as the United Nations Convention on the Rights of the Child. Whatever the final outcome of the consultative process, child care and child protection in Scotland will continue to develop and change within what has become an increasingly international context, due largely to the politics of the process which resulted in the United Nations Convention on the Rights of the Child. Nevertheless, such changes and developments which do occur have to take place within the peculiarities of the Scottish system of child care.

The circumstances of the Orkney Affair, as Lord Fraser suggested, presented the Scottish child protection procedures with a major test. Once again, as in the past, crucial questions have been asked of the Children's Hearings System and it remains to be seen just how far the philosophy provided by the Lord Kilbrandon Committee almost 30 years ago can withstand the demand for change.

REFERENCES AND FURTHER READING

Association of Directors of Social Work in Scotland (1992) *Child Protection: Policy, Practice & Procedure – an Overview of Child Abuse Issues and Practice in Social Work Departments in Scotland.* Edinburgh: HMSO.

Blom-Cooper, L. (1985) *A Child in Trust: The Report of the Panel of Inquiry into the Circumstances Surrounding the Death of Jasmine Beckford.* London.

Blom-Cooper, L. (1987) *A Child in Mind: The Report of the Commission of Inquiry into the Circumstances Surrounding the Death of Kimberley Carlile.* London.

Cleveland Inquiry (1991) *Report of the Inquiry into Child Abuse in Cleveland 1987.* Presented to the Secretary of State for Social Services by the Rt. Hon Lord Justice Butler-Sloss DBE. First printed 1988, reprinted 1991. London: HMSO.

Clyde Report (1992) *Report of the Inquiry into the Removal of Children from Orkney in February 1991.* Edinburgh: HMSO.

Department of Health (1991) *Working Together under the Children Act 1989: a guide to arrangements for inter-agency cooperation for the protection of children from abuse.* London: HMSO.

DHSS (1985) *Social Work Decision in Child Care: Recent Research Findings and their Implications.* London: HMSO.

Draft European Charter on the Rights of the Child (1992). Childright, 88:6–8

Fife Inquiry (1992) *The Report of the Inquiry into Child Care Policies in Fife.* Chaired by Sheriff Kearney. Edinburgh: HMSO.

Finlayson Report (1992) *Reporters to the Children's Panel: their Role, Function and Accountability.* Edinburgh: HMSO.

General Assembly of the United Nations (1989) *The Convention on the Rights of the Child.*

Levy, A. and Kahan, B. (1991) *The Pindown Experience and the Protection of Children. The Report of the Staffordshire Child Care Inquiry 1990.* Stafford: Staffordshire County Council.

Millham, S., Bullock, R., Hosie, K. and Haak, M. (1986) *Lost in Care.* London: Gower Medical.

Newell, P. (1991) *The UN Convention and Children's Rights in the UK.* London: NCB.

Orkney Inquiry (1992) *The Report of the Inquiry into the Removal of Children from Orkney in February 1991.* Chaired by Lord Clyde. Edinburgh: HMSO.

Packman, J. (1991) *Who Needs Care? Social Work Decisions about Children.* Oxford: Blackwell Scientific.

Parton, N. (1991) *Governing the Family: Child Care, Child Protection and the State.* London: Macmillan Publishers Ltd.

Pigott Committee (1991) *Working with Child Sexual Abuse.* London: HMSO.

Residential Child Care Report (1991) *Children in the Public Care: A Review of Residential Child Care.* Chaired by Sir W. Utting Department of Health and Social Services Inspectorate. London: HMSO.

Skinner Report (1992) *Another Kind of Home: a Review of Residential Child Care.* Chaired by Angus Skinner. Edinburgh: HMSO.

SCAFA Report (1992) Orkney Conference Factsheet.

SCLC (1993) *Emergency Protection of Children: a summary of the Consultation Proposals of February 1993, their effect on the existing law, and their sources.*

Scottish Law Commission (1992) *Report on Family Law.* Edinburgh: HMSO.

Scottish Office (1989) *Review of Child Care Law In Scotland.* Report of a Review Group appointed by the Secretary of State, Chaired by J. W. Sinclair. Edinburgh: HMSO.

Scottish Office (1992) 21 *Years of the Children's Hearings.*

Social Work Services Group Statistical Bulletin No. CH 15 1992.

Training Development Group (1991) *Working with Child Sexual Abuse: Guidelines for Trainers and Managers in Social Services Departments.* London: Department of Health.

Vernon, S. (1990) *Social Work and the Law.* London: Butterworth.

INDEX

HMSO publications are available from:

HMSO Bookshops
71 Lothian Road, Edinburgh, EH3 9AZ
031-228 4181 Fax 031-229 2734
49 High Holborn, London, WCIV 6HB
071-873 0011 Fax 071-873 8200 (counter service only)
258 Broad Street, Birmingham, B1 2HE
021-643 3740 Fax 021-643 6510
33 Wine Street, Bristol, BS1 2BQ
0272 264306 Fax 0272 294515
9-21 Princess Street, Manchester, M60 8AS
061-834 7201 Fax 061-833 0634
16 Arthur Street, Belfast, BT1 4GD
0232 238451 Fax 0232 235401

HMSO Publications Centre
(Mail, fax and telephone orders only)
PO Box 276, London, SW8 5DT
Telephone orders 071-873 9090
General enquiries 071-873 0011
(queuing system in operation for both numbers)
Fax orders 071-873 8200

HMSO's Accredited Agents
(see Yellow Pages)
and through good Booksellers

Printed in Scotland for HMSO by CC No 6033   15C   9/93